MYSTERIOUS KEMET

BOOK - I

INTRIGUE AND DRAMA IN ANCIENT EGYPT

S. R. ANAND

MYSTERIOUS KEMET
BOOK - I

First published in 2017.

ISBN-10: 1520568150
ISBN-13: 978-1520568157

Cover Art: Shafali

2 0 1 7 0 2 1 7 1 2

To my readers.

ACKNOWLEDGMENTS

My most sincere thanks to:

Rita and Sid for being the first readers of my stories. Their wise counsel helped the stories grow in both substance and flow.

David Farland for being my mentor from afar and motivating me to publish my stories.

Nancy for being the incredible friend who kept me tethered to my work-assignments that I would have imprudently neglected to lose myself in Ancient Egypt.

My parents for patiently listening to my stories without end, which I told them as a child.

And Bobby, my better half and my most consummate critic, for his patience and love. Without his constant support and his front-line editing, this book wouldn't have been possible.

Thank you!

The Stories

I

A PRAYER TO OSIRIS
~ | FIRST INTERMEDIATE PERIOD | ~

Intef wishes to be Pharaoh, and he would be, if it weren't for his niece Neferu and nephew Mentuhotep. The only way he can win this game of political senet is by winning Neferu's heart and marrying her. But before he can accomplish any of it, Osiris must answer his prayers. What he doesn't expect is that Osiris might give him exactly what he asks for.

II

IMHOTEP'S SECRET DRAWER
~ | OLD KINGDOM | ~

Disturbed by the inexplicable disappearance of someone he secretly loves, Imhotep, the architect and builder of the Step Pyramid, opens the hidden compartment in his work desk and finds something shocking. Left with a gruesome memento, Imhotep must learn a terrible truth about the woman he desires and accept the consequences.

III

THE PHAROAH'S EAR

~ | New Kingdom – Amarna Period | ~

Sunamun, a junior sculptor in Thutmose's workshop, is enamored by the beauty of Queen Nefertiti. When he stumbles upon a secret rendezvous between Thutmose and a mystery woman, he is pulled into witnessing and assisting the power struggle following the death of Akhenaten, which eventually leads him to discover two truths that he must never tell.

IV

SAVIOR OF EDFU

~ | First Intermediate Period | ~

When his lost love beckons, Ankhtifi, the nomarch of Nekhen sees an opportunity in Edfu, which neglected by its nomarch Khuy, has fallen into poverty and anarchy. An elaborate plan, carefully woven into the carnal adventures of Khuy and his mad brother, is executed with finesse. The plan begets its goal and Edfu is saved, but Edfu's gain turns out to be Ankhtifi's loss.

V

THE KEEPER OF SECRETS
~ | NEW KINGDOM | ~

Anen, an artist who works at the building site of Djeser Djeseru is the favorite pupil of Senenmut, the Master builder. He is also the secret lover of Senenmut's mistress. As he toils over the relief of the Punt expedition and prepares himself for the visit of Pharaoh Hatshepsut, a mysterious man turns his life upside down.

Story One

A PRAYER TO OSIRIS

~ | First Intermediate Period | ~

A PRAYER TO OSIRIS

"Tell me now, Mother," he asked, gasping for breath, "tell me before I die. Did I live a lie all my life?"

He lay there, upon the cold stone floor, waiting for an answer; waiting for his mother to tousle his hair, and tell him that it wasn't so.

He heard nothing but silence, ever again.

ⵑⵑⵑ

Prince Intef, fourth of the name, stomped out of Pharaoh's palace. As the white steaming lava of anger spurted within, his muscles bunched up and his handsome face twisted in fury. He had never been this angry in his whole miserable existence of thirty-four years!

Hiding behind the curtains outside Pharaoh's bedchamber, he had learned a truth that made him want to rush into the temple of Osiris, and invoke the god's wrath upon his half-brother the Pharaoh and his nephew Mentuhotep.

May their teeth fall out leaving behind pus-filled abscesses! May their bones crack and break so that they may never leave their beds!

Then he remembered that Pharaoh was already struggling with a mouth full of bad teeth. Unable to chew, he was surviving on soups made of ground vegetables and minced meat.

My curses do come true, he thought. Reinvigorated, he began inventing new ones.

O' Osiris, see to it that their souls never reunite with their bodies. May their bodies rot, for they have given me nothing but pain all my life.

The crown that should have been mine had become his, through a quirk of fate. May he die in pain, with sores on his body!

His thoughts returned to his niece, Neferu. She held the key to his fortune. All she had to do was tell Pharaoh that she wanted to marry Intef instead of that ugly squirt Mentuhotep.

But she hadn't. Curse her too. Curse her beauty. Osiris, turn her into an ugly old hag!

He was the son of Intef the Second, as much as his half-brother Pharaoh was. They shared not just their father, but also their father's name. His brother was the third Intef, and he was the fourth.

There was a time when he didn't mind being called by the same name as his half-brother and his father, but that was long ago, when his father had loved him and his mother. True, he was the son of a lesser wife of Intef the Second, yet by naming him Intef, fourth of the name, his father had acknowledged to the world that he thought as much of his younger son, as he thought of the elder.

Intef's mother was from Nekhen, and she was the most beautiful woman in all of Thebes. His father was already in his fifties when he had fallen in love with her and brought her into his harem as his concubine. Intef was born soon after his mother had moved to Thebes. The rumor that she was a love-priestess of Nekhen was born before he was. When he grew up, he realized that the mean Queen Lah, his half-brother's wife, that stupid cow with the big blasé grin, was behind the rumors.

"She has always hated me. She envies me because she's an empty barrel of wine," his mother had told him.

He hadn't understood the metaphor then, but when he did, he agreed with his mother's assessment.

Intef's father had elevated his mother to the position of a royal wife when he was still budding in her womb. Mother had told him that his father wanted Intef to be his legitimate son and heir!

He had always known that unless his father the Pharaoh declared him the heir to the throne, his half-brother Intef the Third would become Pharaoh. But his mother had Pharaoh's promise that her son would succeed him, and she had repeated it to her son all his life.

But, built on lies, this was a broken family.
Right from the beginning!

Intef the First, his uncle and his father's elder brother who had called himself Sehertawi Intef or "The Intef who had united the two Egypts," hadn't actually united anything! He had loosely strung together a few southern nomes and then proclaimed himself Pharaoh of the two lands.

What a liar!

And when Intef the Second, his father, the lying, deceiving, wretched man had become Pharaoh, he had affixed his bottom to the throne for fifty long years, letting everyone around him grow old as they waited for the old dotard to die. And then, right before he died, the crafty old man, *may his body and soul never meet again,* had played his last dirty trick.

The musty old bag of bones had proclaimed that his elder son, born to his Great Royal Wife, would be the next Pharaoh, and not Intef.

May Ammit feast upon his heart!

He had left the crown *not* to his young, handsome, and

capable son, but to his aging, ugly spawn whose fifty-year-old arthritic limbs creaked when he finally tottered up to the throne and dropped upon it.

No wonder his greedy gnarled fingers weren't letting the crown slip out of his grasp. Pharaoh Intef the Third had spent only eight short years on the throne, when he had taken ill. Now he was fifty-eight and Intef was thirty-four.

It was time that the crown graced the head of a new Pharaoh. Pharaoh Intef the Fourth.

O' Osiris, don't leave me in a lurch again. Help me find what is mine, he intoned.

ᴡᴡ 𓏥 ᴡᴡ

Intef's own palace was the most beautiful building in Thebes. His father had ordered its construction when Intef was born. It was a gift that his mother had asked for, and in those days, Pharaoh seldom refused her anything for he could see nothing past her beauty. He had forgotten his Great Royal Wife, his aging son and his son's aging wife, and he had moved his sleeping chambers to the new palace once the construction had ended.

The new palace, where Intef and his mother now lived, had large airy chambers with high roofs that kept the interiors cool in the hot Egyptian summers. Its floor was made of marble and the walls had scenes of battle drawn upon them, presumably to inspire bravery and courage in Intef. Some of the walls were kept blank, to be filled with drawings that would depict scenes from Intef's life later. The palace also boasted of a garden that had a fountain fed from the waters of Nile and which looked over and across the great river. From the windows of the palace you could watch the sun rise and color the water of the Nile golden.

And yet, all this couldn't hold his father's interest for a very long time. Intef was barely nine when his father suddenly disappeared from their palace and their lives. In those six years that the Pharaoh had spent with them, the palace had bustled with life. Intef would spend his mornings studying history, religion, and writing. In the afternoons, he would practice swordplay with his tutors. His mother often told him stories about his precocity as a child.

But then, one day, his father suddenly left and never returned. He remembered that his mother had cried copiously for a day, but the day after, she had regained her composure and her love for life. The palace was theirs to keep, she had told him.

"Why did he leave so suddenly? And why can't we go to the royal palace and visit him there?" he had asked, plaintively, for he missed his father.

She hadn't answered. He had tried a few more times, but she never answered.

"You will be Pharoah one day," his mother would tell him at least once every day. He knew that she told him the truth. His mother never lied.

He had asked her then, about his father's absence. She had just mussed up his hair and after planting a kiss on his forehead, she had disappeared inside her chambers. He had sat outside for a long time, listening to the sounds that escaped the heavily curtained entrance to her bedchamber, until his curiosity had forced him to get up and sneak a peek inside.

That was the beginning of a new kind of education. Once again, he had his tutor and his swordplay master to thank for it.

The next morning, when his tutor attempted to explain the map of Egypt to him, all he could see on the papyrus were bodies entwined, thrumming, pulsating, pumping – a mad riot of different shades of beige and brown. When he went out into the yard for his lesson in swordplay, he saw his master thrusting and his mother moaning, and he ran back inside, his face streaked with tears.

Things gradually settled down. He learned not to disturb his mother in her bedchamber, and he discovered that despite everything, she loved him more than anyone else in the world.

"Even more than you love father?" he had asked her once.

The absurdity of his question had made her break into peals of laughter. Later when she stopped laughing, she gathered him in her arms and carried him to the terrace from where they could see the Nile in distance.

"You see that river?" she asked.

He had nodded.

"That river is so long that you could spend a whole year rowing a boat trying to get from one end of it to another. And along the river, rise the cities of Egypt," she had explained while he listened, riveted.

"One day, you'll be Pharaoh, and you'll rule Egypt," she said. "And I will always love my Pharaoh, the best."

Her answer had left him confused, but from that day, he had been her little Pharaoh, waiting to grow up so that the double crown could fit upon his brow.

But growing up required time, and time had to be spent. So he had followed in his mother's footsteps. At the age of fourteen, he had already moved to the darker and more private west wing, leaving the east wing for his mother.

Mother and son would go out sometimes, especially on festivals when the occasion demanded that the whole royalty got together. Those were the only times when he saw Pharaoh, his father. He saw him aging and weakening, and wondered when he would pass on the mantle to him. He sometimes wondered why Pharaoh looked neither at him nor at his mother anymore.

"It's because your father is a very busy man," his mother had told him.

It was at one of those tedious royal gatherings, that he had first met Neferu. He was twenty-four then. He remembered that it was the festival of Hathor, and Pharaoh was unwell.

She was a child of eight then, the daughter of his half-brother who was Pharaoh's son by his Great Royal Queen. She had spotted him standing alone and ran across the room to him, her dainty feet pattering upon the stone floor.

"Who are you?" she had asked, giving rise to a wave of nervous giggles and twitters among the women and men who stood there in attendance.

"I…" he crouched down to look into her eyes and placed his hands upon her shoulders, "I am the crown prince of Egypt."

The silence that followed his proclamation was deafening. His eyes slid upon the glassy faces of those who stood there, and stopped at Pharaoh's. The Pharaoh's face looked lean and drawn, and yet he sat alert upon his throne, with the red and white double crown upon his head.

Pharaoh's eyes had swept across the faces of everyone who was in attendance. Intef had hoped to hear his father's voice singling him out, asking him to step forward. Intef had also hoped that his father would remember the promise that he had made to his mother.

He waited for Pharaoh, his father, to speak.

But when he had spoken, he hadn't acknowledged Intef. Instead, in a strong confident voice that didn't match his visage, the septuagenarian had proclaimed that his older son Intef the third would be his heir and the new pharaoh of Egypt.

Intef's world had come crashing down.

That was the first time when the crown of Egypt had been snatched away from him.

The crown that belonged to him was given to his half-brother.

~~~ 𓏏 𓏏 𓏏 ~~~

It had taken him months to accept that he wouldn't be

Pharaoh. After his father had died and his half-brother had ascended the throne, Intef had lost all hope.

He had been twenty-four when his fifty-year-old half-brother had become Pharaoh. If the new Pharaoh lived as long as his predecessor, there wasn't a doubt in Intef's mind that he himself would be hoary and toothless by the time his half-brother vacated the throne for him.

Intef hated old age and old people. He abhorred the old for they made the world look ugly by existing in it. They, with their crinkly skins, crooked bones, and putrid breath, looked and smelled like the creatures of *Duat*. They reminded him that his youth too would flee one day, and he dreaded that day.

Neferu, his young niece, was the opposite.

A few days after their first meeting, she had stumbled into his wing of the palace. She had asked him the question that nobody else ever had before. Not even his mother.

"Why do you live here, in the west wing? It's dark and cold in the mornings and you can't see the river," she had complained.

He could have given her the answer. He could have told her that he hated the bright morning sunlight that streamed in, despite the heavy curtains. He could have told her that the palace was too open and too honest for his liking. He could also have told her that upon turning fourteen, as the tradition dictated, he was introduced to a desire so strong that it had begun to control him, and that the beautiful eastward facing palace didn't allow him the privacy to indulge his desires. But she wouldn't have understood. She was too young to appreciate any of it.

He had given up on Neferu, but she had not given up on him. Not then. For three years since the time he had met her first, the day that old hateful man had given Intef's crown away, Neferu had been enchanted by him. She would sing him the new songs she learned and show him the motifs she embroidered under her tutor's guidance.

Those days, she would visit him almost every week. He remembered having thought of her as a bothersome fly, a pest he wanted to get rid of. He now wished that he had handled her differently. But at that time, he had continued to snub her, again and again; all those times when she would come running to him with her questions, he should have been patient with her. *He could have been patient with her.*

He wasn't because all he wanted then was to spend all his waking hours in the company of those older seductresses!

His memories flitted back and forth, until they alighted on the day when he was in his bed with three of his favorite love-priestesses, the nameless ones. They were three of the most beautiful women in all Egypt, and while steles were raised and walls were painted to extol the beauty of the royal ladies, the true beauties of Egypt were found either on its streets or in the temples of Hathor. Those three were from the streets, and they looked like they came from three different worlds.

There was the golden-haired, blue-eyed girl that came from the North – from beyond the lands of Babylon and Uruk. Her skin was whiter than alabaster and her hair was brighter than gold. He liked her the best, for she reached and touched his body in ways he didn't know existed, and made him feel like a god. Then there was the Nubian beauty. Her skin flawlessly black, her body an exquisite sculpture in ebony, she could make him smolder with desire.

They lay on either side of him, their skin feeling cool and smooth against his, while the third priestess of love, her skin sparkling bronze and her glistening breasts bouncing and teasing, was riding him. His manhood was buried deep within her and he was on the verge of experiencing a release that he never thought was possible, when eleven-year-old Neferu had walked in with a papyrus scroll in one hand and a glass of *sherbet* in another.

He still remembered looking at her standing behind the

swaying figure of the Mediterranean beauty and through the haze of his orgasm he had seen her dazed expression. She had never seen anything like this before nor had she ever seen her favorite uncle in throes of such unrestrained passion. She had stood there and watched, until the woman on top had climbed down, her thighs still slick and slippery. Then Neferu had turned and run away, still clutching the glass of *sherbet* in one hand and the scroll in the other.

Intef shook his head. There was no point in remembering the past.

So what if Neferu had caught him in a love-act? At least it taught her not to break into someone's chambers unannounced. But since that day, she and Intef had grown apart. He should have sensed it then. At eleven she was already nubile – had he done things the right way, he could have made her fall in love with him. But Intef's love-goddesses hadn't trained him to evoke love; only lust.

There were times when he had tried to touch her, hoping that she would react to his touch the way all those other women did, but she had always resisted his gestures. Not that he cared. She wasn't even a woman then, and he was already a grown man. He was twenty-seven and he had needs and desires – like any man would have. Being a prince didn't change certain things.

Neferu had never visited him in his chambers again.

∾∾ 𓊪 𓊪 𓊪 ∾∾

If Mother had not come to meet him, he would not have spared Neferu another thought. It had taken her barely a month to notice that Neferu was avoiding her son. He was seated in his antechamber and eating his lunch, when his mother had swept in, wearing a turquoise linen robe cinched at her waist with a faience belt. As she slipped into a spare chair, he noticed that his mother was beginning to thicken around her waist.

She is aging too, he had thought. It was not easy for him to imagine that one day his mother too would age, or become sick, or even die.

Mother hadn't come directly to her point about Neferu. Instead, at first, she had talked to him about other things.

"Intef, you must take more interest in administration and try to be of use to your half-brother," she had told him.

Administration was a vague word for him. It could mean any of the many things – from managing the construction of Pharaoh's tomb, to auditing the accounts submitted by the nome-governors, to supervising the canal system, to even reading and replying to the messages received from the rulers of the neighboring countries, and there were a hundred things that fell in between. He was a prince, and he wasn't born to work!

But Mother was adamant. Her lips were set in a straight line. The furrows around her mouth further accentuated her unyielding expression. Intef noticed that her skin was beginning to wrinkle around her eyes too. The wisps of her natural hair that peeped out from under her elaborate wig were dyed red with henna. It was odd, he thought, that for many years he had not seen her without a wig. Sitting there with a pearly white shawl around her shoulders, she had lectured him on why it was important that he started making himself useful.

"You are the son of Pharaoh Intef the Second, and after your half-brother's death, you must inherit the crown," she had told him and urged, "Your half-brother is a reasonable man. He will follow the rules of succession."

"I was the crown prince," he had said in a voice full of longing and regret, remembering the time when his father had snatched the crown away from him and set it upon the brow of his half-brother.

"You still can be Pharaoh," said his mother, slowly and emphatically, "and you should be."

It was then that she had finally mentioned Neferu. "If you could make her fall in love with you, nothing else would matter!"

"But Pharaoh…" he had murmured his concern.

"A pharaoh wears the crown. It's true," she whispered, "But it's the daughter or the sister who owns it."

His mother rose from her seat.

"Come with me," she said as she pulled him inside his bedroom and made him stand in front of the tall brass mirror.

"Look at you," she had pointed at his reflection in the mirror. "When a maiden experiences her first flush of youth, she dreams of a man like you. Tall and broad-shouldered, with a face sculpted by Ptah himself! You are the spitting image of your father. All you need to do is, be around her when she steps out of childhood and help her understand her mysterious needs. You can sweep her off her feet, because her young brother would still be a bumbling adolescent then. Marry her before she even begins to think, and win back the crown that your father should have set upon your brow."

He should have taken his mother's advice.

But his sub-conscious resentment for her had returned to nag him, and its roar had drowned her voice.

Am I the spitting image of my father?

His unasked, unanswered question had begun to beat in his head once again.

Am I living a lie?

He had wanted to ask her, but he couldn't. Didn't she tell him every day that he was his father's son and his true heir? Then why did he doubt her? He knew that his headache too would return, soon.

He hadn't heard the rest of it. After she had left, he just sat there, on the edge of his bed with his head in his hands.

Intef hadn't followed her advice, and now he wished he had, even if his life was a lie – even if he wasn't born to be

Pharaoh.

But he was. His mother had told him that he was born to rule; she had told it to him every day of the first fourteen years of his life.

ᜡᜡ ⵑ ⵑ ⵑ ᜡᜡ

The realization of what he had lost by not listening to his mother had hit him like a blinding burst of light, six years later.

He had spent those six years in his palace and on the Nile. He had gone on pleasure-trips to the delta, spending the four glorious months of winter every year in the old necropolis of Sakara near Memphis. The pyramids of the old kings and the temples of love were the two magnificent experiences that Sakara offered to the nobility and the commoners alike. He had just returned to Thebes from one such excursion, when Ineni, his mother's closest aide and favorite eunuch had come to him and announced that his mother wanted to meet him in the east wing.

When he entered his mother's chambers, he was hit by a strong wave of nostalgia. Memories of his childhood, when his father would stay with them for months and the place would bustle with life, assailed his senses.

His mother was sitting in the antechamber, looking older, frailer, and smaller. Suddenly, an emotion that he had never felt before, surged inside him, making him want to envelop her in his arms and tell her that he would take care of her, the way she had, all these years.

Had she? Doubt niggled again.

After the pleasantries, she had come to the point.

"Go and meet your half-brother. He is sick and may not live for more than a year. When he tumbles into the afterlife, you should be there to catch his crown."

So his mother, his sweet and kind mother, had beseeched him to go and meet his half-brother, and he had complied.

Upon entering his half-brother's bedchamber, he had been hit by the smell of sickness that filled the air within. He did not know what had been ailing his half-brother, but the smell had made him want to throw up. He was used to fragrances – perfumes and incenses, and yet he had overcome his revulsion, and approached the bed.

They were already there. Queen Lah, Prince Mentuhotep, and Princess Neferu, along with the royal physician. They stood there, like they belonged. Queen Lah, the fat virago with a pretty face had now transformed into an old harpy with bags under her scowling eyes. Prince Mentuhotep had grown up into a short and stocky young man, who already looked older than his twenty or so years. Then there was Neferu. He hadn't met Neferu for six whole years, but he had heard her name being spoken all across Egypt. Neferu had become Pharaoh's favorite – almost a co-ruler. She handled the foreign-relations, the priesthood, and the nome-administration. Among Pharaoh's four children, she was the only one who would accompany him on his water-trips on the Nile. She was Pharaoh's favorite.

They looked comfortable in the Pharaoh's chamber. Like they came there every day. Perhaps, they did.

Intef, on the other hand, felt like an outsider. His first response would have been to turn and leave, but it would raise questions, and then mother would speak to him. He didn't want to disappoint her, so he had gone in, placing one foot in front of the other without a thought in his head, doing it because it had to be done, not because he had wanted to do it. He had felt four pairs of eyes drill into him, watching his progress across the room.

Why, he had thought then, *why must I subject myself to this?*

Because, his inner voice had answered and propelled him on, *that sick man on the bed has usurped your crown, and you must get it back – for Mother and for yourself.*

As the elder prince and as the true heir of Intef the second, he had a right to the crown! He would give the decrepit old man a funeral that people would gloss over for years to come – all he needed to do was die. When they would embalm him and wrap him in linen, they would place fragrant flowers and jewels in the folds of the cloth, making him smell nicer than he had ever smelled in life. When the old fool died and Intef became Pharaoh, he would magnanimously fill the tomb with everything his dear half-brother would require in his afterlife.

But the Pharaoh was still alive. He lay there in his huge royal bed, looking small and wasted. Intef's eyes became riveted to the skeletal hand that peeked out from under the covers. Oddly, he had been reminded of a day, almost lost in the haze of time, when he had held that finger and learned to walk.

"Brother," he had cleared his parched throat and croaked.

"Shhh…" the doctor had raised a finger to his lip and shushed him up. "Pharaoh is in pain. I've given him the essence of opium to help him sleep."

He had stood there, like a bumbling idiot.

He didn't know what he looked like, but he felt like an imposter. He, the true heir of the Theban Throne, had looked like an outsider.

Perhaps he was an outsider.

His familiar headache had returned to torture him the moment he had stumbled out of Pharaoh's bedchamber.

Was he living a lie?

ᗯᗯ 𓏺 𓏺 𓏺 ᗯᗯ

A year had passed since the day he had visited his ailing half-brother. Today, after a gap of a whole year, he had once again returned to meet the Pharaoh. He had been preparing for this meeting for at least a month, and this morning, he had finally felt confident of being able to present his case to Pharaoh.

True, that he had drifted away from him and rest of the family, but he was not the only one to blame for it. He had gone to the royal palace to set the matters straight.

But he hadn't expected to be faced with such...*such treachery!*

He had heard them from the Pharaoh's antechamber, so he hadn't entered. Instead, he had stopped outside, behind the curtains that separated the bedchamber from the antechamber. Standing there, peeping inside through the thin camouflaged parting between two curtains, he had heard the Pharaoh speak.

His anger erupted once again.

Thirty-four wasted years. After waiting for three-and-a-half decades for the crown and the throne, I get nothing! I get nothing, and that ape Mentuhotep becomes Pharaoh!

His palace was only a couple of hundred yards from the royal palace, but his anger had already tired him out when he dashed up the steps of the west wing. Upon entering his antechamber, he heard the giggles. They were already here to entertain him through the afternoon, but today, the thought of being with them, nauseated him. Not even the most beautiful woman on the bosom of Nut, the goddess earth, could lift his spirits today. Only Neferu could, but she wouldn't. Because he had been a fool! Had he listened to his mother then and tried to win Neferu's love, everything would have been different. But in his heart, he knew that he had lost Neferu the day she had walked in on his orgy.

She was already on the threshold of womanhood when she had stumbled upon him and the women. He remembered that she had filled up in the right places, and her curves were beginning to torture him. He remembered her as she looked then. Her face was already starting to swap its childlike innocence with a young woman's seductiveness. Her lips had become full and red and her eyelashes had grown so thick that they gave her eyes an aura of mystery.

He could have won her heart then. He could have obliterated the scene from her impressionable mind, by casting a different…a romantic impression of himself, instead. He could have followed Mother's advice, but he had been an idiot.

They giggled again. Oddly, he felt repelled by the sound of their giggles. Flustered and angry he strode into his bedchamber. There they were, an array of beauties prepared to enrapture and enthrall him, but he didn't want them.

The crown was slipping out of his reach, and without the crown, he was nothing.

"Get out!" he screamed at them. They spilled out of the bed, naked and bejeweled. Grabbing their skirts and curtsying him, they scrambled out of his bedchamber.

"I will find a way," he told himself as he dropped on his bed. "I will be Pharaoh."

The soft mattress and the fluffy pillows were comforting. He let himself fall back, and then with his feet still on the ground, he spread out and closed his eyes.

The scene from his half-brother's bedchamber replayed in front of his closed eyes. He had watched it from the antechamber, standing behind the folds of the heavy curtain that separated the two rooms.

Neferu was sitting at the edge of her father's bed. It was dark inside and tallow candles burned in the ornamental sconces embedded in the walls of Pharaoh's bedchamber.

In his estimate, since Pharaoh had taken ill, Neferu must have been visiting him every day.

"Where is Mentuhotep?" he heard the Pharaoh enquire, his voice heavy and hoarse with phlegm.

Only when he heard Neferu telling Pharaoh that Mentuhotep was there, Intef realized that his nephew too was inside. When he moved nearer to the Pharaoh's bed and in light, Intef could see him clearly. Mentuhotep was at least a half cubit shorter than Intef and stocky of frame. He had the same permanent scowl on his face that all the Intefs had. All the Intefs, save one. *The whole family was ugly,* all except Neferu who had taken after her mother. They all had square faces and big broad noses. He couldn't fathom why Neferu would marry such an ugly dwarf, when she could as easily marry her tall and handsome uncle.

Suddenly Intef felt acid shoot up his gut.

If the whole family was ugly, why he wasn't?

Neferu too isn't, he told himself, trying to assuage the pain. *I took after my mother, like she did.* But mother had told him that he was the spitting image of his father.

The question returned to torture him once again.

Was he living a lie?

He had torn himself away from the question and tried to focus upon the scene unfolding in front of him.

"Mentuhotep," he had heard the quavering voice of his ailing half-brother. "You must marry Neferu to keep the blood-line pure. She and you are both of the same stock and it's upon your shoulders that the destiny of Egypt now rides."

He had stopped his ears, or they had stopped themselves, for he had heard no more. He had realized that he would never be Pharaoh – not if he didn't act.

To keep the bloodline pure? The blood in their veins was the same as that in his. It was their father's blood.

Hatred welled up within him, pushing him to act the way his mother's words had never done.

He needed a plan.

A plan that would change his destiny and make him Pharaoh. He knew that his mother would stand by him and attest his word, but he needed to act fast.

Intef leaped out of his bed and rushed out to find his guards enjoying a risqué joke. When they saw him they immediately clapped their feet together and stood to attention.

Ignoring them, he rushed toward the east wing to find his mother. He didn't care if this were the time of her afternoon siesta. She would get rid of her lovers and attend to him, the next Pharaoh of Egypt.

〰 𓏏 𓏏 𓏏 〰

Seventy-two days later, Intef and the Grand Vizier stood in the funerary temple of Pharaoh Intef the Third.

Intef was dressed in the finery befitting a Pharaoh. His pleated skirt was fastened with a gold belt studded with precious gems, and his feet were ensconced in soft calf-leather sandals. His side-lock had been shaved off in anticipation. It rankled that he wore neither the *nemes* nor the false beard, but the Grand Vizier Sobek himself had recommended that they waited until the burial. The entire Egyptian nobility and the all-powerful priesthood were expecting Mentuhotep to marry Neferu and become the ruler. Instead, if Intef took over so suddenly, there would be unrest.

So far, it had been easy. Neferu and Mentuhotep must be blind to have not seen through it.

"But Pharaoh is a god," he had tried to reason mostly to keep up appearances, "and they must accept their new Pharaoh with their knees bent."

The portly Grand Vizier had shaken his head and his index finger both with equal vigor. "Don't do that mistake. Let things be done in their correct order. First, lay the dead to rest. Then we will coronate you. The priests will agree to what I suggest, because they know that you'll open the treasury for them. Then you can decide what you want to do with your niece and nephew. Since you would already have become Pharaoh then, the priests will attest your word as divine. But before becoming Pharaoh, if you took one wrong step, they'll side with her."

"She's got them eating out of her palm," he had acknowledged then smiled at the Grand Vizier. "Sobek, you've done a great service to me, and I will not forget it."

The Grand Vizier had given him a courteous bow and smiled back.

"My Pharaoh," he said, "I live to serve Egypt, and will do everything in my power to bring glory to it."

"To serve Pharaoh, and to carry out his word to the letter," Intef had pursued humorously, hoping to get another confirmation from the vizier.

"Yes, to the letter," Sobek had replied ponderously.

"I am Pharaoh," he said.

"Not yet," said Sobek fastening his dark eyes to his, "not yet, but you shall soon be."

The Grand Vizier had forever been a mysterious but exceptionally powerful person, and if he said that Intef would soon be Pharaoh, he would be.

That took a load off Intef's shoulders. He was going to show Egypt that he was the one – the man who had the element of god in him, but for that he must first bury the departed Pharaoh.

And so here he was. A caring half-brother, a doting uncle, and the future Pharaoh helping Prince Mentuhotep perform the opening of the mouth ceremony for his dear departed father. Once his mouth had been opened, the dead Pharaoh would be able to partake of food and gain strength for his journey onward.

After the ceremony ended, there would be a feast, which he knew, would be a tiresome affair. He would head the table and attend to the foreign dignitaries – those who had arrived here to pay their respects to the deceased Pharaoh. He was glad that his niece had quietly accepted his claim to the throne. It was only a matter of time before she also accepted his proposal of marriage and strengthened his claim to the crown and the throne further.

"The priests want you to wear the papyrus sandals for the ceremony," he heard Neferu's voice call him from behind.

He turned, wondering whether it was a good omen or a bad one for him that she appeared in front of him right when he was thinking about her. She stood there, wearing a white pleated linen robe that fell from her shoulders, covered her breasts, and went down to her ankles. The robe was gathered at her waist with a slim faience belt. Her hair was braided with flowers and she wore a garland of lilies around her neck. She looked almost ethereal standing there in the golden glow of the seven candles that were kept lit night and day in the funerary temple.

In that moment, Intef lost his hatred for his niece. He looked at her. She had been crying. She was close to her father, just like he was to his mother. She needed someone who could comfort her. For a fleeting moment he thought of Mentuhotep, the ugly brute she would have married had he not stepped in and taken control. But now that he was going to be Pharaoh, Mentuhotep didn't matter anymore. He would take care of him later.

Intef moved forward and laid a hand on Neferu's shoulder. She didn't shrink from his touch. Emboldened, he raised his other hand and placed it on her other shoulder. His mother was right. They were meant to be together. If she were on his side, the people of Egypt would love him even more.

"Neferu, marry me and be the mother of my children," he said tentatively, prepared to retract the moment he sensed her disapproval. He would have a lot of time to convince her, this way or that.

But there was no disapproval. Not even a hint of it.

She raised her eyes to his and smiled.

"You made me wait for seven long years," she murmured.

Intef was flabbergasted. *Seven years had passed since she had seen him with the love-priestesses. Was he wrong then, in assuming that she had hated him for it?*

He searched her eyes, but all he saw was love.

"Wear the papyrus sandals. The priests are waiting," she said, thrusting the sandals in his hands, before giving him another shy smile and turning away.

Intef thought of calling his servants to help him change his sandals but then decided otherwise. As he bent to unclasp his leather sandals, he felt his erection press against the linen of his under-cloth. A smile spread on his lips in anticipation of a lusty evening in his harem as he remembered the sensation of being with Neferu. Tonight would be the night of celebration.

He had won the most important game of senet.

~~~ 𓏭 𓏭 𓏭 ~~~

Intef turned to change his side and felt sweat trickle down his back.

"Pull those curtains, it's hot in here," he called out still half asleep. His old childhood dream of having lost his way in the desert returned. In the dream he saw himself crawling towards east, where he thought Thebes lay, but he never reached the city.

His eyes flicked open. The darkness was absolute but he was in his bed. He was in Thebes, and he was safe; but it was hot – hotter than it had ever been before.

And the servants hadn't followed his order. They hadn't drawn the curtains and it was still pitch-dark. His chamber was never completely dark, he recalled. All through the night, two lamps burned in his bedchamber. And that wasn't the only thing that felt odd and unfamiliar. He touched his bed and ran his hand over the sheet then he reached out for the pillows. The sheets were of silk and the pillow was made of dove-feathers.

This wasn't his bed.

He was sleeping in a different bed that was far more luxurious than his own. And then he remembered. He was now Pharaoh – or he would be the next morning. He remembered everything in bits and pieces. He had returned from the opening of the mouth ceremony – tired but elated, and instead of going into his chambers in the west wing, he had run up the steps to the Pharaoh's chambers. He had lounged in the antechamber for a while, sampling the figs and grapes from the silver bowl imported from Byblos. He had then asked the women to be sent in – they were a selection of whores that had been brought in from Uruk.

Despite the heat and discomfort, he felt his excitement rising. He reached down to feel the throbbing weight and began comforting himself.

His thoughts once again returned to the previous evening.

He remembered lumbering into the Pharaoh's bedchamber and falling upon the bed, waiting for the women to arrive. His memories of the latter events were vague – but he did remember seeing a glimpse of paradise through a haze of beige and gold. He remembered a mysterious but erotic perfume that he had never smelled before, and then some giggles…and finally, a familiar but unexpected voice.

Intef felt his excitement drain. He went limp in his hand, as his concern deepened.

Why hadn't the servants arrived yet?

He had to do something – or this darkness would devour him.

He got up and swung his legs down the bed. His leather slippers were right where he had expected to find them.

Intef slipped his feet into the slippers and called the servants once again. His temper was now rising.

Where were they? And why the heavy curtains were drawn close?

At night, if at all, only the muslin curtains were drawn as they allowed the moonlight and the breeze in.

He tried recalling the layout of Pharaoh's bedchamber. It wasn't easy, because he seldom visited his father.

"Where were those lamp-sconces?" he murmured, trying to focus on what he remembered of the Pharaoh's chamber.

The pictures began forming. He saw himself outside the Pharaoh's bedchamber a week before his half-brother's death. Neferu and Mentuhotep were inside. The sky had already darkened outside but Pharaoh's chamber was lit bright with a dozen lamps. Two of the wall-sconces carrying these lamps were right near the headboard of the Pharaoh's bed.

Intef turned left. Moving against the edge of the bed, his outstretched hand touched the wall. He moved his hand up along the wall. There it was. Now he needed a flint-lighter.

Where could he find one?

He tried focusing on his memories again. Perhaps they would help him locate the lighter. In his imagination, the Pharaoh's chamber lit up again.

Where in the name of Osiris were the servants? What was the point of being Pharaoh, if you couldn't have two servants at your disposal?

He bellowed again. There was no answer. *Something isn't right*, he thought as his voice echoed through the place.

He ran his fingers around the edge of the sconce once again. They hit something. *The lighter.* A wave of relief washed over him. His fear of darkness was quite recent. It started exactly seventy-two days ago. It had been dark when he had stolen into this very chamber that night and poisoned the jug of water that stood on his half-brother's bedside table. The explosive mix of anger, jealousy, hatred, and fear had driven him to kill his half-brother, the King, the Pharaoh of Egypt. And since that night, he had been afraid of the dark. But now, he thought, I must not be, because his half-brother was already on his journey into the world of Osiris, the god of death, and he had felicitated

Osiris and offered him sacrifices so that his half-brother were given comfortable quarters and would experience no desire to return from the dead.

He released the clasp of the flint lighter and put it to the wick of a lamp. An unearthly yellow glow filled the chamber. Intef heaved a sigh of relief, and set about lighting the other oil-lamps.

Tomorrow he shall punish those servants. Hanging them with Mentuhotep will be a good idea.

"But Mentuhotep will die only after he has seen Neferu get married to me, the new Pharaoh of Egypt!" he chuckled, wiping the sweat-beads off his brow.

The lamps burned casting a steady glow. There wasn't the faintest flicker in their flames.

He pulled a sheet from the bed and wiped his face and neck.

"Let me draw the curtains myself," he whispered, and walked to the eastern wall, where the windows were.

There were no windows.

He stood facing a wall that was painted in blue, yellow, and gold - a wall that told the story of the Pharaoh's rule. Blood drained from his face and he felt a chill run down his spine. Very slowly, pivoted to his spot, he turned again.

His half-brother's sarcophagus, hewn out of a single block of marble and inlaid with gold and precious jewels, stood proudly in the center of the chamber.

Intef looked around. A flask of wine stood against the windowless wall and a sled-table laden with fruits was placed next to it. He remembered the layout of the tomb and ran to the entrance, but the entrance had been sealed with a slab of granite that weighed about two tons. The air inside was in limited supply. The thought made him panic.

Nobody knew he was here, he thought. This had to be a mistake.

Who would do this to the Pharaoh? Who was present at the closing of the tomb?

Everyone!

But who prepared the tomb for the closing? Who brought in the items for the Pharaoh to use in his afterlife?

The priests, the Grand Vizier, Neferu, and Mentuhotep!

"Neferu!" he muttered. It had to be her, for none of the others would have either the courage or the intelligence to come up with such a plan. It was suddenly all clear to him. Nobody outside would miss him – and they all got what they wanted.

Except Mother! Mother would leave no stone unturned to find her son. All he had to do was survive until then.

The thought strengthened Intef and calmed him down. He turned down the wicks of all the lamps except one. Until Mother discovered that he was missing and came looking for him, he had to survive, and it would be foolish to fritter away the light.

He knew that mother would find him, but he would invoke divine intervention from his favorite deity to help her. He fell on his knees and closed his eyes. The image of the green god holding the crook and the flail swam in front of his eyes.

"Osiris, I've served you all my life; I've been your son on earth. I promise to raise the biggest temple for you yet. Osiris, let my mother find me."

He prayed fervently, recalling all the instances when Osiris had heard his prayers, until behind his closed eyes, he saw a benevolent smile spread upon the face of the god.

And then he heard a rustle of fabric. It came from the treasury – the smaller room annexed to the burial chamber, in which all the things that Pharaoh would need in his afterlife were kept.

Before he could turn to go and check, he heard his mother's voice.

"What is wrong with the servants, why are the curtains

down?"

Osiris had heard his prayers.

〜〜 ﻉ ﻉ ﻉ 〜〜

Historical Notes:

During the First Intermediate Period, the governmental machinery in Egypt failed, and two distinct power centers emerged – one in the South (Thebes) and the other in the North (Henen-nesut, later called Herakleopolis.)

Intef the First, or Sehertawy Intef, was the nomarch of Thebes who grew in power and proclaimed himself the King of Egypt. He established the 11th dynasty, which ruled from Thebes.

His brother Intef the Second followed him, who was in turn followed by his son, Intef the Third.

Nebhepetre Mentuhotep, who was the son of Intef the Third, married his sister Neferu, the eldest daughter of Pharaoh Intef the Third, and reunited the Upper Egypt and the Lower Egypt, bringing the First Intermediate Period to an end and becoming the first Pharaoh of the Middle Kingdom.

Story Two

IMHOTEP'S SECRET DRAWER

~ | Old Kingdom | ~

IMHOTEP'S SECRET DRAWER

This expanse on the east bank of the Nile was a place frequented more by robbers and wenches than the nobles of Memphis. The priests, however, were omnipresent, and they could be found even among the riffraff, presumably to bring light to them and lead them to the gods. This was why Imhotep the great builder and the future Grand Vizier of Egypt sat on a rock that overhung the river, clad in the robes of a priest.

On the opposite bank, far out on the southwestern horizon, he could see the silhouette of the stone quarry. Nearer, right on the bank of Nile, antsy looking fishermen were pulling their nets back and preparing to end the day. On the waters were some papyrus boats, most of them near the west bank. A single barge bobbing up and down upon the rather peaceful surface of the river was ponderously making its way toward the other side, apparently disdainful of the scrounging scum that thronged this bank.

Imhotep turned his attention to the glass vial that he held in his hand. It was about a palm width tall, within which was the gruesome relic that she had left for him. He looked at it. The cork had ensured that the smell didn't escape the vial, but the shrunken crinkled skin covering the limp little piece of flesh and the two wrinkly sacks attached to it, couldn't be mistaken by anyone.

〜〜 ⑂ ⑂ ⑂ 〜〜

As evening fell upon the Necropolis, the shadows began to lengthen and the bright whiteness of the desert started turning into an ashen gray. Imhotep sat on the cool floor of the verandah of his house, and watched the pyramid. It was still a pyramid only in his imagination. It was going to be a stepped structure with four sides that would converge at the top, and in doing so it would still imitate the form of a pyramid.

The huge pyramid that was supposed to help the King ascend into the heavens was but a small part of the complex that Imhotep was building. Around the pyramid was the enclosure wall, outside which was the trench that had supplied most of the stone blocks used in building the pyramid. Then there was the South Tomb, which thankfully was already done, and the southern colonnade that would lead to the enclosure. *It is still a work-in-progress,* Imhotep sighed then turned and went inside.

The antechamber of his house was a neat square room with white walls. Against the wall on his right stood a life-size statue of Ptah, the patron god of artists, artisans, and engineers. Carved from cedar imported from Gubla, across the Sinai Peninsula, the statue was a gift from his King. It was his most expensive and cherished possession. On his left was his table, where under the watchful eyes and the protective gaze of Ptah, he would sit perfecting his designs, calculating dimensions, determining angles, and deciding upon the most effective way to construct the tomb complex that would facilitate King Netjerikhet's passage into the afterlife.

Imhotep went back to the design he had been working on. The papyrus roll with the drawing was laid across the top of his low sled table. It beckoned, *no,* challenged him to build it. He had meant to make the sides look toward the sky, shiny and reflective, so that regardless of the position of the moon, the pyramid could always be seen. He had also wanted it to be a lot taller, but the King was already disquieted by the new structure. It was true that it deviated from the flat-roofed mastaba tombs that were in vogue, but they didn't make the kind of statement he expected the pyramid to make. Unfortunately, Imhotep still hadn't been able to come up with a formula for the planes on the side.

He picked up the tumbler and downed the liquid in it. It was water with a hint of *bhang*, an herb that was imported from Babylon.

Imhotep was twenty when he had been assigned to work on King Netjerikhet's final resting place. Now he was nearing thirty. In the past ten years, he had not just designed this Pyramid, but he had also written about thirty scrolls on illnesses of the human body and their remedies. It was one such illness that had brought him close to the King.

When the King had begun to suffer severe bouts of stomach cramps, Imhotep had offered to help. He had palpitated the King's stomach and by studying his winces and groans, he had diagnosed that the King had developed little wounds in the lining of his stomach and intestines. He had then prescribed him a concoction of herbs to be taken along with a goblet of warm goat's milk, twice a day. In three days, the King's agonizing pain had been replaced by mild discomfort, and in seven days, he was once again devouring his favorite dish, the inner-thigh of Nile's water buffalo stuffed with boiled corn and cooked in lamb-fat.

Since then, Imhotep had risen not just in the King's

estimation, but also his affection. He was often called in the King's chambers at odd hours, sometimes just to play *senet* with the King of Egypt. Had Imhotep played even half as well as he could, he would win every game, but he was smarter than that. He would play just well enough to make the game challenging and then lose at the right time. Intelligence and smartness were not the same thing, he would often tell his pupils, but he had a feeling that most didn't know what either meant.

As he sat on the floor sketching and calculating, the sun began to set behind the structure that he was building. The workers were slowing down, the supervisors were not flicking their whips often enough, and all of them were waiting for the Sun to go home, so that they could too.

He was so lost in his work that he didn't see the golden glow of the afternoon sky give way to the cold gray of an Egyptian evening. Only when he heard her voice, was he brought back into the present.

"It's time to stop work. Your bath is ready."

It was impossible to ignore Neith's call, partly because her voice could soften the hardest hearts, and partly because Imhotep's stomach was beginning to demand succor.

"A few moments…" he lingered over his work, trying to quickly scribble down his last thoughts. He might yet find a way to get those tiles to fit perfectly on the inclines of the stepped pyramid.

Neith sat down upon the mat that was meant for Eni, his assistant. He had hoped, despite all the ominous signs he read in the stars, that Neith and Eni would fall in love and raise a family together. Neith was eighteen, credulous and nubile and at the point in life when a young woman can be taken advantage of, especially, a young woman as beautiful as Neith. His thoughts now turned to her. He watched her as she gathered his papyrus scrolls, her soft yet firm arms going around the rolls and holding them close to her chest. She was of a light-brown complexion.

A dash of white from her mother, who was a slave from the northern lands, had lightened her Egyptian brown complexion and given it a golden hue. Her eyes slanted upward at the corners and her eyelashes were dark and thick lending her an air of mystery. Her red full lips could make a man dream about things…

Imhotep shook his head. The thought made him angry. He was Imhotep, the man who would soon be the Grand Vizier of the great and undivided land of Egypt. Rich men of every ilk would trip upon one-another's feet to marry their daughters to him. If he wanted, he could fill his house with wives and concubines, and their children, but he didn't. He had searched his soul for an answer, again and again…but he had come up against a wall – a white wall with a false door. The kind of doors he was building in the enclosure wall of the tomb, the ones that never opened, at least not in this life.

He stole another glance at her. Her shoulders were speckled with beads of perspiration that caught the evening light and shimmered as she moved. Below her young firm breasts, she wore a linen skirt that went down to her knees. It was wrapped around and tied with a slim leather belt that he had painted for her. In the waning light of the setting Sun, she looked beautiful. Inadvertently, Imhotep let a sigh pass his lips. She raised her eyes and caught him watching her.

"What's wrong? You look worried," she enquired. She had already stacked his scrolls neatly and capped his inkbottle. Now she sat with her feet tucked beneath her and both her hands folded neatly in her lap.

"Some measurements are not adding up," he replied, hiding his real thoughts. It was true that he was worried. At her age, a hundred things could go wrong. Perhaps, it would help if he spoke to Eni's father, who was a merchant of linen in Memphis, and got them married. Once she was married, no harm could befall her. She and Eni could live here, under his protection until she became a mother, and even after, when her hair would turn gray.

But she would still remain as desirable, wouldn't she?

Once again, he found himself unable to think beyond her marriage. *How would it solve my problem?* He thought.

"So is Eni staying for dinner?" he asked her trying to keep his voice indifferent.

She gathered his rolls in her arms and stood up, her lips curving in a smile.

Imhotep, who was a man of science, turned into a blundering fool when it came to matters of heart, and he knew it. Neith was the opposite, and she liked to come directly to the point. He knew that she was going to ask him something — something that would put him in a spot.

"Why should you, the architect of the King's tomb, the greatest mathematician, physician, and thinker of Kemet, play the matchmaker for a poor girl?" she asked, smiling impishly.

Imhotep smiled despite himself. For a moment, he wanted to let the burden of his false pride drop off his shoulders. For a moment, he wanted to be Eni, a scribe who would not have to answer to the King if he married below his station. *If I weren't Imhotep, I would make her my wife,* thought Imhotep. Her father was a mason who was working on the pyramid and Imhotep was sure that he would not have refused.

"So it's not Eni who makes Neith blush. Who is it then?" he enquired, secretly hoping that she would blush at the question and avoid answering it. Instead, she held his gaze then slowly turned and walked away.

Imhotep watched her hips undulate and sway under the thin linen sheath that she wore, and cursed his obsession with her.

Outside the house, night had already chased the evening away. The dark sky was studded with stars and a half-moon was pinned upon its southern part. The mastabas were spread upon the chest of the desert far into the north, their silhouettes rising only slightly against the deep purple of the horizon. The pyramid of Netjerikhet would be different though. At eleven hundred and seventy seven *meh niswt*, a unit of measurement that roughly was the length of a man's forearm from elbow to his middle finger, it would rise higher than every other building in Egypt. It would be a monument deserving to be the tomb of the greatest ruler of Kemet. Imhotep looked at the number and smiled. Adding the figures until a single figure was obtained as the sum, eleven hundred and seventy seven resulted in the auspicious seven. He also had no doubt that the stepped pyramid that he was building would change his destiny.

And yet, despite everything that he did or had, he wasn't happy – not in the full sense of the word. He spent most of his waking hours working for the King, but when his day ended and he went back into his private chambers, he felt alone. He could make a pyramid to let the gods know where they would find the *ka* of the King, but he couldn't understand why anyone would want to reach the afterlife and be reborn? A part of him wasn't even ready to believe that there was an afterlife. He knew that when he died, they'd make a tomb for him too, in which they'd lay his mummified body. Of course, his tomb won't be as rich and elaborate as a king's, and it would possibly be somewhere out in the desert, but that would be fine, because Imhotep preferred to be alone. Except in those moments when he wanted someone to lie beside him – someone who would cradle his head between her breasts and plant a kiss on his head. *Someone like...*

He shook his head again.

The girl was taking control of his senses. He couldn't let that happen. He was Imhotep; he controlled all that could not be controlled by the gods or the kings. He would never let anyone or anything control him.

More than three hours had passed after dinner when the hour of midnight approached, and Neith stole out of the house. Her father lived in the barracks of the workers, but Neith had a special place in Imhotep's household, a room near the kitchen that belonged only to her.

Between the South Tomb and Imhotep's house lay the entire tomb complex. The path that diagonally cut through the complex would have been much shorter, but it would also have exposed her to the guards, so she ran along the boundary-wall, using the shadows as her cover.

Upon reaching the South Tomb's entrance, she looked around to check if anyone had seen her. Nothing looked out of place. She rushed through the dark corridor that led to the stone steps, which descended into the burial chamber of the tomb. They had completed the construction of the South Tomb last year and while Imhotep's stepped pyramid would take a few more years to be completed, the King was already beginning to age. The South Tomb would serve as a temporary resting place for the King if he began his journey to the afterworld earlier than expected.

There were almost a hundred steps and though they were paved with stones, the debris still hadn't been removed. It was heaped on the sides, narrowing the steps some more. The painting of the two walls flanking the steps had not yet begun. For the last two lunar-phases, work had completely stopped in the South Tomb, which meant that there could've been no better place for their rendezvous tonight. As she descended the steps carefully, her hand pressed to the wall, she remembered Imhotep.

He was worried about her, this much was clear. He was interested in her as a man would be in a woman, this too was clear, because when he looked at her, his eyes were filled with longing. She had often seen him watching her. Imhotep was a handsome man. He was tall – about a head taller than her and had a straight nose and a hard, chiseled face. When he was intent upon a problem, his lips would set in a straight line and his brows would furrow over his deep dark eyes that didn't reveal much. But what his eyes didn't reveal, his actions did. He was overly protective of her, and while his actions had irked her before, going down the dark steps into the sepulcher, today she saw merit in them.

He doesn't want me to fall in love beyond or beneath my station, because all such love brings is pain, agony, and despair, she thought. She knew it now, but there was little she could do about it. She had fallen in love, already. She had also hurt herself, worse than Imhotep could ever imagine.

Below, but still a few cubits ahead, she saw the entrance glow bright against the dark well of the staircase. The smell that wafted up and the flickering edge of the circle it threw upon the ground told her that the light came from a torch burning lamb fat. Focusing on the light ahead made her lose her balance and she stumbled, missing a step, but her hand shot out and she placed her palm against the wall to stop her fall. The misstep made her miss a beat and for a few moments she stood panting, waiting for her breath to normalize.

The sound she made must have alerted him, because she saw his silhouette appear in the mouth of the tomb. Her heart beat faster with each step she took.

Inside the chamber, little reflections of the torch's flame bounced back from each little faience tile on the wall, turning it into a sheet of shimmering liquid. The faience on its walls used to create the mosaic that depicted scenes from the life of the King, and the colors had sprung to life. This was where the King's body would be kept while his tomb received its finishing touches. She had once given it a name that had made Imhotep smile. "Tomb of the Traveling *Ka*," was what she had called it.

As soon as she stepped inside, he wrapped his arm around her shoulder and walked her into the door that connected to one of the inner chambers. As she loosened her muscles and allowed him to steer her, Neith was still unsure of her feelings. She had heard about prisoners falling in love with their captors. Perhaps it was the same with her.

"Are you fine?" he asked, his voice comforting and gracious. He was always polite. In the beginning, she had not been able to see through his veneer of politeness, but gradually she had learned the truth that everyone in Egypt already knew – the truth that Prince Nebmakhet was an exceedingly cruel young man. They told stories about the punishments that he had meted out to those who had displeased him. A boy of four who had picked up a date from the bowl meant to serve the prince had lost his tongue so that he may never taste anything ever again; a man who was in love with a woman who had caught his fancy, was cut into seven pieces, and all his pieces, including his head were displayed around them while the prince had taken his pleasure with the woman. Those were the stories that she heard, hidden behind an expressionless face, for she couldn't tell anyone how well she knew the villain of their stories.

Until now, fortune had favored Neith. When Nebmakhet's rapacious eyes had first fallen upon her, she was just fourteen. She had been his hidden concubine for the last four years. In these four years, she had realized that she had not given herself to one man, but to two. There were times when he was a lover who brought her flowers and perfume, and who shared with her intimate secrets that she knew he never shared with anyone else, and then there were times when he turned into an oppressive maniac who raped her for hours because he experienced an indecent pride in sustaining his arousal.

She had loved him, feared him, hated him, and despised him. She knew that she hadn't experienced the full wrath of his fury, perhaps because she had never crossed the boundary.

Once. Perhaps.

Once Neith had almost crossed the boundary, and asked him about the unsavory rumors. At first, her question had made him angry. His face had turned hard like it was hewn from granite, but soon that look had dissolved into a smile. He had pushed his head in her lap and told her that she shouldn't let rumors sway her, and that he never meted out punishment to anyone who didn't deserve it. His answer had made her skin crawl, and from that day on, she had promised herself that she would never question his past again.

Tonight, she wanted to ask him a question, but it would have to wait. First, she will have to play along. His answer to her question would decide her future, and yet, whether she would be able to summon the courage needed to ask the question and then to accept his answer, remained to be seen.

"Remember the day when I had first seen you?" he asked, slowly removing her linen shawl from her shoulders, and letting it drop upon the sheepskin that was spread upon the ground.

"Yes," she murmured. She remembered the day, and also the night that followed. In a haze of pain, she had lost her virginity that night.

"And the night?" he asked, like he was reading her thoughts.

Her fear returned, making her shiver. Silently, without moving her lips, Neith prayed to all the gods whose names she could remember.

He pushed her down on the sheepskin rug and unclipped her skirt. Neith knew the ritual as much as she knew the reason why she must not do anything until he asked for it. Years ago, at the beginning of their relationship, she had once attempted to unhook his *shenti,* only to have her hand angrily slapped away. She still remembered the look on his face when he had rasped, "only whores do that. I love you because you aren't a whore."

So she lay there upon the rug, shivering and waiting. The tomb was more than fifty cubits below the surface and it was cold in the crypt, but she shivered not just from the cold that her skin soaked up from the air and the ground, but also from a dark and ugly secret that she held hidden inside her chest.

"I'll warm you up," he said, his smile turning into a leer as he removed his gold belt, his *shenti*, and then his thong. Standing there naked, he looked like a god, the stark opposite of what she now knew him to be. His bronze skin that covered his muscular body sparkled and glistened where the light from the lamp bounced off it. Nebmakhet, unlike the other royal scions, didn't confine himself to the pleasures of the palace. He sought and found his happiness outside the white walls of the royal residence, in the streets of Memphis, on the sands of the desert, and upon the wild waters of the upper Nile. He was built more like a warrior than a prince.

With each breath that he took, light cascaded down and rippled upon the muscles that clad his torso, his thighs, and his hips. Below his muscled abdomen rose the stele, its hard and shiny surface encasing a pulsating, throbbing monster, ready to force its way into her and tear her apart. She looked at it and trembled for she had experienced the pain it could cause.

"You know something," he whispered into her ear as he fell upon her, thrusting his raving member inside her, her involuntary resistance causing it to chaff her and make her sob. "In a week from now, I shall be on my way to becoming the king and a god. Let me in and make me feel like the king and god that I will become."

A mixture of fear and comprehension loosened her muscles and he slipped inside - pushing, beating, pulling, and tearing, he continued to hammer into her for an intolerably long time. Kneading her soft body with his callous hands, chaffing her delicate skin with his furious but loveless need, and using her fearful cries of pain as his fuel, after an interminably long time, he thrust himself into her one last time, after which he lay upon her spent and panting.

Then he rolled off her and lay supine at her side.

She glanced at him sideways. His eyes were closed, but she knew that his senses were alert.

"Neb," she whispered.

"Hmm," he nodded, waiting for his breath to normalize.

"Will you marry me?"

Nebmakhet wasn't King's son. He was the son of King's brother. Everyone in the realm knew that the only way he would ever ascend the throne could be through his marriage with princess Inetkaes, the only daughter of the King. Like him, there were other suitors too; and unlike him, they were closer to wooing the heart of Inetkaes. One among them also had the King's approval, which Nebmakhet didn't have. King Netjerikhet had made it clear that a man with Nebmakhet's reputation would never marry his daughter, nor would he rule Egypt. This meant that Nebmakhet was free to marry anyone he chose. He did rule three nomes in the name of the King, and he had promised an innocent and trusting Neith, that when time came, he would marry her.

In the beginning, Neith had trusted him implicitly, and when the poisonous snake called doubt had raised its terrible head for the first time, she had already learned to fear him.

They had met four years ago, when the work on the pyramid had begun in earnest and the King had paid a visit to the site. Nebmakhet had accompanied the King as his other courtiers had. On the fateful evening, Neith had been called to fill in the shoes of the lead-singer who had fallen ill, and she had become the cynosure of the program. The fallout was that Nebmakhet had seen her.

Several nights later, he had abducted her. Unlike the

other royals, Nebmakhet liked to operate alone. "The only way to keep a secret is to do the deed alone," he had told her on more occasions than one. For the first three years in their relationship Nebmakhet had told her on each of their meetings that he would marry her and make her a princess. In the last whole year, he had said it not once. Neith had gone through the pain of his lovemaking and the ignominy of their nocturnal trysts with the hope that she would one day be his wife - a lesser wife perhaps, but one with her own chambers and maids, and that she would be able to get her father to give up masonry and live with her.

"What did you say?" his question suddenly drew her out of her thoughts. "Nothing," she was afraid to repeat her question. But he had heard her, and then he told her about his plan.

She knew about the revolt. The news-runners who came to Imhotep had already brought the news that in Upper Egypt, a revolt had begun. Led by Prince Khunum, the revolt aimed at dividing Egypt once again.

What she didn't know was that Nebmakhet had another plan that would run in parallel to the revolt and ensure that King Netjerikhet was interred here in the South Tomb before the next full moon, and Nebmakhet himself would be married to Princess Inetkaes.

"Will she marry you?" she asked, still in shock.

"The priests will make sure she would. The gods will speak in my favor," he laughed harshly.

"If you marry the princess, you will be the king," she said haltingly. A king could have many wives, and yet, they usually married a woman from their family or from nobility. As a prince, Nebmakhet could have married her; as the king, he would never.

There was a time when she had loved him, with her heart and her soul; worshipped him with her body and her mind...

"Will you..." she began, her voice quavering with fear.

"Marry you?" He completed her thought and laughed again. "Marry you? You are a whore with a magnificent body and an angelic face. A queen has need for neither, but she must not be a whore."

His reply wasn't unexpected, yet his words sliced her heart and slashed her dreams. Until now, she had been hanging from a thin thread of hope. His cruel words had broken that thread, and by breaking it, he had strengthened her resolve. She had been preparing herself for this moment, and now it had arrived.

He propped himself up on his elbow, and gave her a long, hard, and searching look. She didn't allow her pain and anger to appear on her face and smiled. Inwardly, she cringed. Her heart flailed and battered, she wondered how a woman who had always remained true to a man and who had first been taken by him against her wishes, could be a whore.

She knew that the next part of the ritual would involve his quaffing some wine, but before that he would empty his bladder. He would go out into the burial chamber and water the area where the King's body would lie, should he die before the pyramid was completed.

Neith watched him rise and walk out of the low door. She waited to hear the tinkle of his water hitting the ground, and then she sprang up and bolted across the room to the lone tool rack that stood against the opposite wall. Her heart beating painfully against her ribs, she felt the ground under the rack. Her fingers hit the vial almost immediately. The tinkle still continued. She darted back and emptied the vial into his wineskin that he had flung aside before they had made love. She tied the mouth of the wineskin again and threw herself upon the rug. As she lay there, steadying her breath, she could hear the steady tinkle give way to the sound of those last few drops falling on the ground.

He stooped and entered through the low door once again. She lay there, still naked, just as he had left her. He liked her to be naked when he drank his wine, sloshing some of it on her thighs and licking it off. Not always, but sometimes, when he was less drunk, this would result in another bout of lovemaking, less violent and painful than the first, but equally disgusting to her.

Tonight, it would be different.

He dropped down beside her and reached for the wineskin. She raised herself up to help, but before she could, he had already picked it up.

Untying its mouth with a flourish that comes with practice, he looked at her.

"You don't hate me for it, do you?"

She did. With all her heart and soul. But she shook her head.

"I am a whore, and I know it," she murmured.

He took a large sip from the wineskin and pulled her to him.

"I hope you are not. You are *not,* are you? Have you been with another man, ever?" he asked her, twisting her wrist and making her wince.

She thought of the times when she had wanted to be with another man. Tonight she regretted not knowing him because she found herself wishing that she had. She wished she had given herself to him, even as his concubine, because he was kind and considerate. He wouldn't have given her pain. He loved her, she knew. Only he wouldn't show it. But he would have loved her and cherished her forever. A faint memory of Imhotep bandaging her finger when she had cut herself, slid past her open eyes. That sweet feeling of having been cared for had lingered on, comforting her on days like this.

In the year past, she had hoped that he would say something. He hadn't. She didn't know why, but whenever she had returned from the South Tomb, raw and aching all over, she had gone to bed thinking about him, imagining his arms around her, touching her and caressing her, kissing her pain away.

Now she knew why, but it didn't matter anymore. She didn't deserve to be loved, for her heart now carried only fear and hatred.

"You didn't reply," he said, still twisting her wrist and pinning her down with his leg and chest, the monster once again throbbing against her thigh.

"Never," she replied, truthfully. *Never, but I wish I had.*

He swung the wineskin to his lips, gulping down and guzzling half its contents. She watched him without blinking. She didn't want to miss anything, not even the smallest twitch.

Now it won't be long before the poison took effect – it would numb his muscles but not his capacity to feel pain. She had read Imhotep's scroll on the subject.

When his grip on her loosened, she knew that it was time. She slipped out from under the weight of his knee and picked up her leather belt.

"You can't be leaving already? I haven't given you permission to leave," he said, haltingly.

"No, I am not. I won't leave until we are done," she replied, pulling out the bronze-blade from the hand-painted leather pouch pendant that hung from her belt.

Fear rushed into his eyes when they caught the glint of bronze on the sharp edge of that palm-long blade.

"What are you doing?" he asked, alarmed, as he tried to raise himself up but flopped back.

"Taking away what you won't need where you are going," she said with her voice unnaturally calm. Then kneeling against him, she raised her leg and swung it across his chest pinning him down to the ground.

His eyes widened with fear and his throat became parched as comprehension dawned upon him. He tried to raise himself up but his body refused to respond. As the poison was absorbed in his stomach and spread through his body, it paralyzed him.

She scooped it all up – his limp member and his testicles, and then she lunged at it with her blade, hoping to hack it away. But the blade's edge wasn't sharp enough to slice it in one clean stroke, so she slashed again, and again. Perhaps the gods wanted her revenge to be spectacular. With each stroke, white pain shot through his loins and ran through his spine. His screams rebounded from the walls, echoing and multiplying in their intensity, yet never leaving the crypt to reach outside.

With each new gash, blood sprung forth, splashing upon her and painting her lovely face and naked body crimson, while he squirmed and screamed in a red haze of pain, unable to move, until life began to ebb out of his body. As she sat there watching him die, she felt the soft white muslin of peace descend upon her. After he had taken his last breath, she rose to her feet - a dreadful vision streaked in red, and started the preparations.

ᗯᗯᗯ ⎝ ⎝ ⎝ ᗯᗯᗯ

The next morning, she wasn't there.

Imhotep began work on his drawings once again. It wasn't easy to calculate the exact dimension of each of the polished limestone tiles that would cover the stones. They needed to abut so close that not even a hair could be laid between two of those. It was a royal specification, which couldn't be sidestepped, but even if it were possible, he wouldn't, because Imhotep was a perfectionist.

When he lifted his head, Ra had already done half his day's work and was shining right above the heads of the workers who he could see from where he sat in the verandah. Their shrunken shadows told him that it was exactly noon.

Everyday exactly at noon, she would arrive with a glass

of pomegranate juice for him. She had done it without fail, all these years. He felt the pain of her absence more acutely than he had ever felt the comfort of her presence.

I took her presence in my life for granted, Imhotep thought. But then what was a man supposed to do? At first, she was a child and his indulgence was avuncular, then she surprised him by growing into a lovely young woman, who made him question his own feelings. How was he to manage his conflicting emotions? And then, there was the matter of pursuing his ambitions. He cared for her and that made him consider questions that would never cross the mind of another man.

Care? Or consideration?

I don't even care enough to name my feelings for her, he thought. *It's because she is younger than me,* he reasoned.

His reasoning made him chuckle. Examples of mismatched marriages abounded. King's youngest wife was a third his age, and Eni's father had married a girl half his age when he had crossed thirty-five. He could do the same, except that he couldn't disappoint King Netjerikhet, nor the lords who wanted him to marry their daughters. Staying unmarried was his way of ensuring that he didn't ruffle the feathers of all those old ostriches whose approval could be the difference between his achieving his dreams or disappearing from history. They understood his devotion to his work and smiled indulgently when he spoke of being wedded to the quest of knowledge, but he was sure that they would never understand his taking Neith for a wife.

And he wouldn't subject Neith to being his concubine.

But none of it meant that he could stop thinking about her. Her absence was like a thorn in his heel. He had to pluck it out or the pain would not allow him to work.

Perhaps he could speak to her father, the mason; or the cook, because she spent a lot of time in his house – studying, fussing over him, and helping the servants with the chores. She had arrived in Memphis with her father about ten years ago, when he had announced the construction of the new pyramid. Many had come. They had arrived from everywhere, hoping to get work in one of the construction projects in the Necropolis.

He tried to busy himself with the drawings and calculations, but his heart wasn't in it. *It's time to confront the truth,* he told himself. *I should go and talk to her father.*

"Lunch is served," he heard the announcement, but it was made by Eni and not Neith.

He turned his head and looked at Eni. He was a good-looking young man, healthy and well groomed, and he was a scribe. There weren't many scribes in Egypt. Hieroglyphs had been around only for a few hundred years and the kings were beginning to realize the importance of preparing for their afterlife only now. And yet, Imhotep knew, that this was the beginning of a new age – the age of tombs and pyramids, and scrolls and steles. Egypt had been trading with the lands nearby and sending its ships across the sea. In this age of sharing and recording knowledge, being a scribe was a really good thing.

If only Neith chose Eni, she could live in Imhotep's house forever. Married to Eni, she would never leave. Once again, Imhotep felt that familiar squeeze on his heart as he thought of Neith being married to Eni.

After dismissing Eni he pushed the drawings away and went into the living area, where his lunch was already laid out on the low sled-table. The fruit-bowl was filled with succulent slices of figs and crimson seeds of ripe pomegranates. A bronze flask filled with goat's milk stood proud and tall, inviting him to take a swig. Six boiled duck-eggs peeled and sliced in the middle, were arranged on a wooden plate. He took his place at the table, and the servant girls silently pattered out to serve him. He waved them away. He could serve himself, unlike most other noblemen in the kingdom. The lifestyle of the rich in the kingdom was fast becoming tainted by their untamed desires. While Imhotep could afford to live a life of similar unrestrained luxury, the prospect of it failed to excite him. He lived for the satisfaction of solving problems, and he knew well that a quest of his kind would fail equally at stimulating others.

The lunch was a quick affair. He preferred to eat less in the afternoon because a full stomach slowed him down. The servant girl brought the water bowl for him to wash his hands. Imhotep went through the motions mechanically. The question that had been harassing him since morning returned to haunt him.

While he was still trying to decide whether or not he should speak to her father, the reed-mat on the door was flung aside violently, and a young boy who he recognized as one of the royal runners, stumbled in.

The guard rushed in behind the boy.

"I tried stopping him, but he said he wanted to see you," he tendered his excuse, which Imhotep did little to acknowledge. His attention was upon the boy. "What was so important that it couldn't wait?" he asked.

"A missive from the King, my Lord Imhotep," he said curtseying by almost doubling up as he handed him the scroll with the royal seal.

Imhotep calmed the boy down and asked the servants to feed him. Inside his work-chamber, he broke the seal and unrolled the papyrus on his table. The King wanted to see him about the possibility of a revolt. This was nothing new, but what caught his attention was the glyph that symbolized the palace. *The King was anticipating a revolt from within.*

Nebmakhet, he thought.

The ambitious young prince whose claim to the throne was so tenuous that it was almost non-existent, wanted to be the King. Surrounded by a coterie of sycophants, his cruelty had earned him the name *Metut,* or the poisonous semen of Seth, the god of chaos.

Though Imhotep was not a military man yet the King thought highly of his ability to propose solutions to all kinds of problems. He knew that the King needed to consult with him urgently, or the runner would not have been in such a tearing hurry. He would leave tonight. In an hour, at most two, he would be in Memphis. He could spend the night in Memphis, and meet the King early morning tomorrow.

The feeling of emptiness, however, refused to leave him. Every year, she went to Memphis with her father or with the servant girls who worked in the kitchen but at this time, there was no festival in the city, and he was sure that she would have told him if she were going somewhere. She wasn't ill or she would have sent a servant to him with the news. Something wasn't right, but he, Imhotep, couldn't ask, nor go looking for her. And yet, he knew in his heart that his trip to Memphis would result in new responsibilities, and might even take him away on long trips to the cities in the outer nomes of Egypt for he may need to garner the support of the nome governors.

But before he left, he wanted to see her and talk to her at least once. The need to see her was so strong that for a moment, he stopped and thought about the futility of all that he had accomplished or was going to achieve in the future.

Could any of it bring him that little wisp of happiness that he so desired?

Imhotep, the man who was considered a genius, the man at least half as famous and revered as the King himself, couldn't do anything to comfort his heart, because every moment of his was watched. The King was always suspicious of everyone and that included his wives. Two of his lesser wives had gone missing, and the grapevine had it that they were found discussing a young man from the kitchen, making salacious remarks upon his physique, and the King had come to know of it. Since then, the wives weren't heard of. They might be in one of the dark cellars that were constructed a hundred years ago by King

Narmer, the first king of all Egypt.

If only he were a lesser man, he would have married Neith and raised a family with her. But now, as one of the most influential and powerful men in Egypt, his destiny, even his choice of wife, lay in the hands of the King.

What price must a man pay for following his dreams? Imhotep asked himself as he absently slid open the drawer of his sled-table.

He had designed and fashioned this table himself about nine years ago, when they had started constructing this tomb for the King. That was also the time when Neith's father had first arrived, part of a group of men and women who had traveled to Sakara from the far eastern reaches of the kingdom. With her mother dead, nine-year-old Neith shadowed her father everywhere. Even on that day she was with him, holding his index finger in her fist. Her innocent brown eyes flitting from one thing to another in the antechamber – she hadn't seen anything like it before. Imhotep had given her father the job of the assistant to the mason and sent the young girl to the kitchen, where they could feed her and find some work for her.

But she hadn't stayed in the kitchen. She was a precocious child, willing to learn and experiment. If she were a boy, Imhotep would have trained her to be a scribe.

He looked at the open drawer, and memories flooded back in. It was her drawer. She had designed it. Well, almost. When Imhotep was making the table, she had been sitting by his side, watching him work. When he began fashioning the drawer, she had suddenly lit up.

"Can you not make a secret drawer?" she had enquired.

Of course, he could, but he asked her – wondering if the child could really solve the problem, "how would you design it?"

She quickly explained it to him – the idea of inserting a panel to create a false back that flushed with the base so that it seemed attached to it, and a hole to put in a hook, which could be used to pull the panel out.

He had made a little secret drawer at the back of the main drawer, and she had been using it. Its contents had been changing though. At first they were trifles and toys of a child. Then a small bronze mirror that he had gifted her, appeared in it, along with a few shell combs. Later when she had begun to paint her eyes, the contents of the compartment had changed into a kohl-box with two containers, one for galena and the other for malachite, and a couple of brushes. Then four years ago she had stopped hiding her things there. Imhotep had attributed it to her growing up. Today, missing her presence for the first time in the last nine years, Imhotep felt a strong urge to open it once again.

He found a piece of electrum wire and fashioned it into a hook. Then he squiggled the head of the hook inside the tiny hole that was visible only if one knew it was there. A slight tug and the drawer rushed out. Inside it was a glass vial, and a small papyrus roll.

He sat there in shock, looking at the contents of the vial. There was no mistaking the shrunken skin and what it might be. It was an ugly token that he found impossible to associate with the innocent beauty and the sweet disposition of the girl he knew, and yet, nobody else could have placed it here.

With his heart thundering against his ribs, he reached out for the papyrus scroll and unrolled it.

It contained a name, a sketch that looked like the plan of the South Tomb's inner chamber, and a heart-rending request. He sat there looking at the piece of papyrus for a long time and then replaced it in the drawer. Then he picked up the vial, covered it with a piece of linen he used for soaking up the extra ink from his reed pens, and walked with measured steps into his bedchamber.

Inside, the great Imhotep flopped upon his bed allowing tears to well into his eyes. He sobbed silently reviewing the equation of his life, wondering why he, with all his brilliance, failed to balance it. He had sacrificed the only thing that mattered, by ignoring his feelings for the only person who ever made him smile. He had condemned himself to a loveless existence so that he may build tombs for the unfeeling, unsmiling dead.

Imhotep had carved out his heart and placed it upon the altar of his ambition.

᚜ 𓈗 𓂀 𓂀 ᚛

He stood inside the inner chamber of the South Tomb, holding a torch that burned with an ochre flame, imbuing the crypt with a ghostly glow. It was middle of the afternoon and yet inside the tomb it was pitch dark.

He remembered that about two weeks ago he had detailed the South Tomb construction team to work on the Pyramid instead. The South Tomb was almost ready. If the King chose to leave the world early, only a week would be needed to clear up the debris and prepare the tomb to be the King's temporary resting place, until his Pyramid was ready to receive him.

The place looked just the same as it did on its last inspection, but because he knew where to look, he dropped to his knees upon the floor, which was never made – it was just raw earth and dirt. This inner chamber was situated behind the burial chamber and when a tall man stood inside, the top of his head brushed against the ceiling. The room was just a cavity in the wall to store the tools and push the debris in, during the construction. It would later be filled with stones and bricks, and sealed off. He wondered why he hadn't ordered it to be filled up yet, for the work on the tomb was finished and there was no need for this chamber to exist anymore.

Absently he wondered whether Neith would still be alive, if he had ordered this chamber to be filled up.

Probably not. Fate doesn't dance to our tunes, we dance to hers, he thought.

In the light of the torch that he had brought along, Imhotep carefully checked the floor on the left side of the door through which he had entered. The surface was damp and he knew why, but there was nothing that would give anything away. Neith's letter was clear and direct, just as she was. Nebmakhet and his seditious thoughts were buried there. He wondered how much Neith knew of Nebmakhet's ambitious plans. She had not mentioned them in her letter.

Unknowingly perhaps, Neith had rendered Egypt a great service. *She had saved the King.*

Imhotep turned his attention to the ground on the right side of the entrance. The dirt here was loose. She had tried to bury herself in, but there was no way for her to pat the loose dirt back upon her dying body. Painful visions of Neith trying to bury herself flooded his imagination. First, he saw her digging her grave, then drinking the remnants of the poisoned wine that she had used to kill her devourer, and finally, sliding into her eternal bed. Then he saw her waiting for the poison to take effect as she tried to cover herself with as much dirt as she could.

Neith, who had flooded his life with sunshine, lay half-buried in a dark, unnamed tomb.

He brushed the sand off her face and sat there looking at her, reciting verses, and invoking the gods to bless her journey into the afterlife. Crying silently, he made her a promise – a promise that he would keep until the last day of his mortal life, until he would join her in the afterlife.

As he buried her, he imagined her sweet innocent heart on the weighing scales of Anubis, far lighter than the feather of Ma'at.

For a fleeting moment there, Imhotep had turned into a believer.

As he ascended the steps, he pulled himself together.

There was a lot waiting to be done, for the dead were now at peace, but the living still clamored for their share of misery.

Tomorrow, he would issue the order for filling up the chamber.

ᗯᗯ 𓏤 𓏤 𓏤 ᗯᗯ

He threw in the lamb-pieces first. The great river was home to many water-creatures. The huge hippopotamuses, which were revered for their closeness to the river goddess, the fish – small and big, and the crocodiles that were feared and avoided by the Egyptians, for they had no sense of territory. They would crawl and even gallop upon the banks with the same agility that they displayed in the water. They were the reason why Imhotep was here. Every Egyptian knew that if they devoured a part of a body, in the afterlife, the person would be born sans that part.

The pieces he threw into the water attracted them to the spot. Within a few moments, they were already swarming under the water, only their scaly shiny backs visible. Imhotep took a long breath, placed a curse on the ominous thing in the bottle, then he uncorked it and upturned it, letting its contents fall into the congregation of crocodiles below. He watched the surface of the water break into swirls and splashes, as jaws of all sizes swooshed out, snapping in the air. He watched the piece being snapped up by one of them, while the others thrashed about disappointed.

Buried without his terrible accouterment, Nebmekhet would never again be born a man. If scriptures were to be believed, he would forever search for it in his afterlife.

The first and last task that she had set him was done. Imhotep would never love again.

He looked at the vial in his hand and then returned it to

the pouch that hung from his waist.

It was night already, and tomorrow he had to meet the King.

〜〜 ⏐ ⏐ ⏐ 〜〜

Historical Notes:

Imhotep designed the Step Pyramid or the Pyramid of Djoser for King Netjerikhet of the third dynasty (who later came to be known as King Djoser) at Sakara, ca. 2630 to 2611 BC. The purpose of building the South Tomb has never been established clearly.

In addition to being considered the father of all architecture, Imhotep was also a physician. Eminent 19th-century British practitioner Sir William Osler considered him "the first figure of a physician to stand out clearly from the mists of antiquity."

None of the historical texts speak of Imhotep's marriage.

Around the time of the New Kingdom, Imhotep was deified, and was spoken of as the son of Ptah, the patron god of builders, architects, artisans, and artists.

Story Three

THE PHARAOH'S EAR

~ | New Kingdom – Amarna Period | ~

THE PHARAOH'S EAR

Upon the west bank of the Nile, a farmer was tilling his land. His wife sat upon a rock singing a song, waiting for him to finish his work so that they could return to their adobe hut together. The farmer stopped every now and then, and listened to the song his wife was singing.

You are my Ka, my Amun, my Ra…

It had been difficult for them to let go of their old gods that were everywhere - in their songs, their prayers, and their dreams. But the farmer and his wife had followed their Pharaoh and tried hard to accept Aten as the only god, and yet it was difficult to assume that just one god could accomplish so much. *How could he have created the whole universe, including the Sun, the Moon, and the Earth? How could one god make sure that the flow of Nile never stopped? And how could one god preside over the entire cycle of birth, life, and death?* It was all a lot simpler when there were many gods, each dedicated to a task, each with a characteristic story – you knew exactly which god to evoke and ask for help when you faced a problem.

The farmer wiped the sweat off his brow and stopped to listen. He liked this part of the song. It was about Nile…and love.

> *When you touch me, I come alive,*
> *You kiss me and make me fertile,*
> *Without you, I am a dry desert,*
> *Your touch makes me Kemet.*
> *You are my Ka, my Amun, my Ra…*

He looked across the Nile. In the golden light of the setting Sun, the palace looked beautiful, like it was hewn out of solid gold. It had large windows overlooking the river, and in one of the windows, for the last many years, there had been a lone figure of a woman. For the last six months, the window had been empty.

> *But someone was there today.*
> *Not a woman, but a man.*

~~~ 🜔 🜔 🜔 ~~~

The announcers had come in the afternoon. They came beating the drums followed by a long procession of the royal criers accompanied by the harpists, the percussionists, and the singers of the Hymns of Dead. After raising a stele in the center of the city, they had left. The stele claimed that Pharaoh was dead. It was indeed a sad day for Egypt, for Pharoah wasn't just their ruler, he was their father, and in this case, he was also *the one closest to Aten, the only god,* for all the other gods had been banished by Pharaoh Akhenaten, when he had made this new city Akhet-aten.

The many gods of the past had been left behind in Thebes when Amenhotep, fourth of the name, or Akhenaten, as he had later begun calling himself, had disowned them to proclaim Aten as the only god and moved the capital of Egypt north, where he had raised this new city he had named Akhet-at-en. The sculptors and the builders who had come along hadn't expected the Pharaoh to die so soon, but he had, even when his tomb was still under construction.

Inside Thutmose's Workshop, the air was heavy with fearful anticipation. The stone-chippers, the sketch-artists, and the sculptors were all at work, but their faces wore expressions of uncertainty and concern. They had to finish the tomb statuary in time for the burial so they had to work, but their movements were mechanical, and the murmurings were anxious.

Thutmose was in the administrative wing, a set of three rooms sandwiched between his residence to its north and his famous workshop to its south.

The most important and the biggest room in his administrative wing was his work-chamber where he met his sculptors and reviewed their work. This was an odd room, for it had four doors, each for a different Thutmose. His artists and sculptors came in through the door that connected his work-chamber to the Sculpting Workshop. That door was meant for Thutmose, the perfectionist.

The door in the opposite wall, the one behind his work-table, connected to his house, and was for Thutmose, the family man, who was a husband and a father.

He received his patrons, the nobility of Akhet-aten in the antechamber, which had an entrance from the King's Road. His rich patrons would alight from their litters and walk straight into a room that was almost as richly furnished as their own homes. There, he had on display some beautifully sculpted heads, busts, and full-length statues of men and women, young and well formed, and quite unlike his own clientele. His porcine patrons would place their meaty bejeweled fingers upon the sculpture they wanted theirs to imitate, pay him the advance, and waddle out with dreams of an afterlife in which they would be born as perfect specimens of humanity. The door that connected his work-chamber to the antechamber was for Thutmose, the statesman.

The third room was his private space, a bedchamber of sorts. It could only be accessed through the fourth door of his work-chamber. It was a room with a curtained window and a bed that stood pushed against its far wall. He retired to it for a few hours every afternoon. The door to this room was for Thutmose, the man he was.

It was still not afternoon, but this was the room where Thutmose was, and he was not alone.

〰 𓏏 𓏏 〰

Sunamun dashed across the courtyard of the workshop, stubbing his toe on the corner of the pedestal being used by a new sculptor struggling to get the likeness of the human face and who had so far succeeded only in making it look like a baboon's. Half the artists who worked in the open courtyard of Thutmose's Workshop were already in, chiseling away. He was late.

Thutmose's Workshop was a large complex with a hostel for the junior sculptors and the artists, the storerooms, and the sculpting court that could be entered from the King's Road. The hostel rooms were situated on the right of the entrance and the stores were on the left, to the north of the court, close to the administration wing where Thutmose's work-chamber was situated.

His stubbed toe was aflame with pain, but he ignored it. The agony that Thutmose would inflict upon him would be far worse. He would bar him from refining the features of his granite sculpture of Queen Nefertiti and punish him by asking him to prepare the roughs. The roughs were head forms hewn out of different types of stones. The senior sculptors then used the roughs to chisel in the facial details. While Sunamun was very young and had spent not more than two decades on earth, he was already chiseling details and was on his way to become a senior sculptor. He knew, and so did Thutmose, that given a few more years Sunamun could outperform the Master Sculptor himself.

The ignominy of being relegated to the task of doing the roughs was bad enough, but if the material for the roughs was…

"Oh Aten, let it be anything but quartzite," Sunamun prayed under his breath. He had seen the fresh sculpting material that had arrived from south, and it was mostly quartzite and some limestone. Limestone was a lot easier to work with, and if he was going to waste his time chipping away mindlessly, he hoped it would be limestone. Quartzite gave him nothing but blisters.

As he ran up the steps of the stores area with his toe throbbing, he was reminded of how big Thutmose's workshop was. He had heard that the workshops in Thebes were even bigger and grander, but he hadn't seen them. He was from the delta and grew up in Memphis. This was another matter that long back, Memphis itself had been the seat of the Egyptian royalty, and the first pyramids were built nearby in Sakara. But those were old times. He and his friends often played near the pyramids in winters – and while the elders often spoke about the old pharaohs and considered them divine, they thought of their current pharaohs as human – and Akhenaten certainly was considered a heretic king, not only in Thebes and around, but also in the delta.

Thutmose had found Sunamun next to the pyramid of Khafre, where he was sculpting a discarded piece of limestone into the head of Hathor for his mother. "Your place is in my workshop," he had told him. Then Thutmose had gone along with Sunamun to meet his destitute parents and sought their permission for taking him away to Akhet-aten. Sunamun's parents had only been too glad to send their fourth son and seventh child with Thutmose who had promised to take care of their annual supply of grain, for as long as Sunamun worked in his workshop.

On his left was the room where their tools were stored. On the right, there were two smaller rooms: one stored the paints, and the other, semi-precious stones that were imported from faraway lands. Right ahead was the door to Thutmose's work-chamber. He caught his breath and slowed his step.

Sunamun was about to the lift the papyrus reed mat hanging from the top edge of the door and enter, when he was halted by hurried whispers that he heard inside. As the whispers grew louder, he recognized the voice of the Master Sculptor. The other voice belonged to a woman. He strained to hear the conversation but the sound of his own heavy breathing interfered with his hearing, and he could catch nothing more than some stray phrases.

"Nobody must know," said the voice of a woman.

"Nobody will. But you must go back and tell…" replied Thutmose.

Silence followed, disturbed only by some faint sounds that were oddly out of place in Thutmose's office. The voices piqued Sunamun's curiosity. He wiggled out of his leather sandals and tiptoed to the door where he lifted the papyrus mat slightly and peeked inside.

The work-chamber where he had often stood in front of Thutmose's desk was vacant. At least a dozen gypsum casts of heads at various stages of completion crowded the Master sculptor's worktable, which was surrounded by wooden stools. The workbenches along the walls of the room looked equally busy with anvils, casting boxes, and sculptures of royalty, but Thutmose wasn't there.

However, it was now clear to Sunamun that the sounds were coming from the room on the right, the private chamber of the Master Sculptor.

He dropped the edge of the reed mat and pressed his ear against it. His effort was rewarded with the soft rustle of linen, followed by the sound of skin slapping against wet skin. He heard moans and cries of pleasure, followed by the controlled but ecstatic groan of a man experiencing release. Standing there, listening to the sounds they were making, he felt a rush of pleasure that began by flushing his face and then washing over his shoulders and his abdomen, it finally reached his loins.

Sunamun lost his sense of time. All he wanted now was a quiet corner, where he could be alone for a few minutes. So when in his daze, he heard Thutmose's voice, a loud whisper, his heart skipped a beat and his legs almost gave way under him.

"Go back to her. Tell her that everything will be fine."

Sunamun took a few steps back and tried to steady himself. He had to meet Thutmose for his work details, but he didn't know if he could risk meeting him now.

The sounds of the rustling fabric and the creaking bed had abated much before he heard footsteps inside the work-chamber. The woman was leaving through the antechamber of Thutmose's office.

Then he heard the regular everyday sounds in the work-chamber - a stool being dragged, the busts being moved, and a sigh of exasperation. It sounded like Thutmose was reviewing a piece of sculpture that didn't meet his approval.

Sunamun took a long deep breath before lifting the reed curtain and requesting permission to enter. Thutmose was already seated behind his huge cluttered desk, correcting a cast, his steady hand drawing unwavering lines that would later make the sculptor wonder why he couldn't see his errors earlier.

Thutmose didn't lift his eyes from his work, but nodded, signaling him to enter.

"You are late," he growled.

For a moment, Sunamun reflected upon the irony of Thutmose's remark. He was sure that his early arrival would not have met Thutmose's approval today. Yet his characteristic growl sounded right, as it always did for Thutmose always growled at everyone – the sculptors, the painters, the water-bearers, the stone-chippers. He had even been heard growling at some of his rich clients who wanted him to make their *ka*-sculptures for them.

But he wasn't growling a few minutes ago. In fact, he sounded excited, even enraptured, and yet, Sunamun mused, *completely in control, as always.*

Thutmose was a handsome man - tall and dark, with musculature that could put a horse to shame. Most sculptors weren't built like that, and by the time they had put four decades behind them, they had either earned enough to live out rest of their lives in villas that overlooked the Nile, or were still toiling over the statues of rich men and women, their lungs calcified with the lime dust they inhaled as they chipped away the stone. But Thutmose was different. His smoldering eyes set deep under his straight dark brows arrested the onlooker's gaze, seldom allowing it to appreciate his strong cheekbones and his square jawline.

This was the reason why the stories that were told only in the dark of the night and under influence, all sounded true, for why would Queen Nefertiti who was fabled to be the most beautiful woman in entire Egypt, not want to have such an incredible specimen of masculinity as her paramour, when her life was tethered to the effeminate and gangly Pharaoh?

Could the woman that Thutmose was with, be the Queen? Sunamun thought, stealing a look at the door that led into the private chamber of Thutmose. It too was covered with a reed mat that hung from its top edge. Sunamun had stolen a glance inside once, a long time ago, and he knew that the Master Sculptor kept a bed inside. He shook his head and tried to focus on the matter at hand.

"Apologies, My Lord. The carriage I rented this morning was owned by a miser who didn't feed his horses well, and so one of the horses fainted…"

"Spare me the details of your trials, Sunamun. Some urgent matters need my attention, and I need your help," Thutmose cut him short and motioned him to sit. Sunamun was taken aback by the Master Sculptor's unexpected gesture. But it was not his place to question his mentor, so after dusting a thick coat of gypsum powder off a stool, he perched himself upon it.

"More than forty days have passed since Pharaoh died," mused Thutmose, scratching his chin. Sunamun noticed the stubble and waited. Something had been troubling Thutmose, and it wasn't just the death of the Pharaoh.

"We had moved here with Pharaoh Akhenaten and in doing so we had aligned ourselves with his ideology. We accepted his theology and told the world that we believe in Aten and only in Aten," said Thutmose, still intent on the gypsum cast of a middle-aged woman's head. He ran his thumb over the brow-ridge then marked it to be chiseled off some more.

Sunamun leaned forward to ask a question, but Thutmose held out his hand, stopping him from speaking.

"The problem now is, we don't know who the new Pharaoh would be. Tutankhaten is very young, barely six, and Pharaoh has left no other male heir. These are uncertain times. While Lord Ay, the Chief Vizier and Pharaoh Akhenaten's maternal uncle would guide the new Pharaoh, we must wait and watch."

Sunamun listened. He would turn twenty in a few months, and he had never given the royalty much thought except for Queen Nefertiti, and even then his thoughts had been mostly adulatory for he was infatuated with her. He could spend all his life sculpting the face that had enamored him and taken his imagination hostage.

He kept his feelings to himself and tried to concentrate on the twisted royal relationships. Though he hadn't met any of the people Thutmose was speaking about, he knew who they were.

Tutankhaten was the sickly young son of Pharaoh Akhenaten from a junior wife. With his Chief Royal Wife Queen Nefertiti, Akhenaten had produced only daughters. Akhenaten's Chief Vizier Ay, now a man already past his middle age, was not only the Chief Vizier, but also Akhenaten's maternal uncle. It was also said that Nefertiti was Ay's adopted daughter. In Sunamun's opinion, Queen Nefertiti could be Pharaoh, for Egypt already perceived her as the pharaoh-in-waiting.

"But what about Queen Nefertiti?" Sunamun enquired. "She could be our next Pharaoh, couldn't she?"

Thutmose pushed away the head he had been correcting, and looked straight into Sunamun's eyes catching him unawares.

"Would you like her to be?" Thutmose pinned him down with his piercing eyes.

Of course, he had wanted to say clearly and emphatically, but Thutmose's glare froze his words in his throat, and he could manage merely a nod.

Thutmose noted the nod. "Then you must help," he said. "I need you to do something, but before I tell you what, you must promise not to speak a word about it to either the living or the dead."

Thutmose's words had an odd effect on Sunamun – they scared and excited him at the same time. "I promise, not to tell. Neither to the living nor to the dead," he said, his voice quavering slightly.

He seldom spoke with the living, let alone the dead, and for a promise so simple to keep, if he could be of service to Queen Nefertiti, Sunamun wouldn't flinch. *Who knew, he might even get the opportunity to talk to the Queen.*

ᴧᴧᴧ 𓈖 𓈖 𓈖 ᴧᴧᴧ

That night, Sunamun did not sleep. His conversation with Thutmose had left him excited and anxious, and for the first time in his whole life, he found himself thinking about something other than sculpting.

More than a month had passed since Pharaoh's death, and while the official mourning would last for seventy days and end only after the burial, the new Pharaoh hadn't been announced yet.

Rumors abounded among the rich and the poor alike.

Some thought that Tutankhaten, Akhenaten's son had the right to wear the crown, but if Tutankhaten became Pharaoh now, his maternal grandfather Ay would become the regent. Nefertiti had already co-ruled Egypt with her husband for almost two years now. As a sculptor, he knew that Akhenaten had always considered Nefertiti his equal, for the royal edict for sculpting the royalty clearly specified that Pharaoh and his chief royal wife should be rendered almost equal in size.

For the people of Akhet-aten, it didn't matter who wore the crown. What mattered was that in the city of Akhet-aten, they had learned to live a different kind of life. They had chosen to live under the protection of a single god, Aten. He had heard that while everyone else in the royalty had accepted Aten, whenever Ay traveled to other nomes, he still sought the blessings of the old gods. Nefertiti would keep Aten and their city alive, they were sure of it, but nobody knew what Ay would do, if he became the regent.

Sunamun tossed and turned in his bed, unable to sleep, as his mind was an untidy jumble of thoughts. Just last evening, a discussion in the dining hall had taken an ugly turn, when Pinhasi, another sculptor from Thutmose's workshop, a burly man of middle age, half in his cups, had banged his fist upon the table to make a point.

"Nefertiti will be Pharaoh," he had screamed, pounding upon the table, scattering the food and making the beer-tumblers fall. Most of the others cheered because they loved her. They had been copying her bust for the last seven years, and they all felt a strange connection with Nefertiti. So most of them agreed, except a few.

Ifeyni, a junior sculptor who had arrived from Thebes just a couple of years ago, was a staunch supporter of the old gods.

"She cannot be Pharaoh. Not only she doesn't have the divine element in her, she also doesn't care for our gods. Look where Pharaoh Akhenaten, *may the gods forgive him,* brought us. We are in the middle of nowhere. Our beautiful Thebes with its busy streets and magnificent temples has been left behind. Returning to Thebes now remains our only option, and she will never allow that."

Sunamun had disagreed with Ifeyni silently. He thought that Akhet-aten was a beautiful place. It had the potential of growing into a great city with its own temples, palaces, and markets, even its own necropolis.

He hoped that Nefertiti would become Pharaoh. She had been at her husband's side through everything. She was with him when they had arrived here from Thebes and laid the foundations of this new city Akhet-aten; when they had built the temple of Aten; even when they appeared in front of their subjects.

And I hope I'll be able to help, he thought.

Sunamun found it impossible to sleep. His mind had transformed into an arena where opposing thoughts fought to gain his attention. He got up and swung his feet down, feeling the floor for his slippers. He found them. Slipping his feet into them, he got up and walked to his window. It was a full moon night and the pilasters in the sculpting court cast long mysterious shadows upon its floor. They appeared to be hiding something, just like Thutmose was.

Thutmose was his Lord, and even though Sunamun wasn't Thutmose's slave in the records, he knew that his love for sculpting would keep him in Thutmose's thralls forever.

Sunamun could not shake off the feeling that something was not right, but it wasn't his place to question his employer. He checked out the stone water clock that stood in the center of the courtyard. In another hour, he would start out for the Royal Workshop where Thutmose had said he would meet him.

He picked up the flint lighter that lay in an alcove next to the window, and lighted a candle, which he placed upon the table. His small table was a busy affair. He kept his tools there, along with a jug of water, and his drawing-scrolls. In the middle of the table, stood the bust of Nefertiti. The bust wasn't his creation. It was the Master Sculptor's. It was meant to be a reference to be used for sculpting her statues in limestone, quartzite, even granite. Every sculptor in the Workshop specialized in something – sculpting hands, sculpting torsos, fitting tenons into mortises; Sunamun specialized in sculpting Queen Nefertiti's face, and this was why the reference bust stood upon his table.

He sat down upon the edge of his bed and looked at the bust. The light of the sole candle cast an ethereal glow upon it, accentuating its colors and its shadows. Almost a cubit high, the bust represented the neck and the head of Nefertiti, with her tall blue crown perched upon it. The bust had a limestone core upon which layers of stucco had been added to refine the features. A golden band and a Uraeus coiled around it, protecting the wearer. Nefertiti's bust had a faience pectoral imitating strings of flowers, around her slender neck. Her symmetrical face, her feminine yet strong jaw, and her full lips often made him wonder whether Thutmose had made her more beautiful than she actually was. And yet, this reference bust had a flaw. Its left eye was never completed. It was a hollow, painted in white, waiting to receive the stone that would bring it alive. Sunamun knew that the wait was eternal, for the socket of the left eye was meant to be empty. It allowed the sculptors to determine how deep they must create the hollow, so that the eye could be replicated faithfully.

Her name, Nefertiti meant, "the beautiful one has come." In his room, in the small hours of the morning when the whole world slept, *the beautiful one* belonged to him. Thutmose had handed the bust over to him six months ago, and in those six months, he had fallen in love with Nefertiti. It was true that she was the Queen of Egypt and that there was only a chance in ten thousand, that she would ever notice him. Yet he had the right to dream, and so dream he did. Every night, he would look at her lovely face before he went to bed, and then he would dream of her. Often his dreams would spill into his night, waking him up and making him wonder why such a beautiful woman must sleep in the bed of that terribly ugly man?

The lines of her face and her lone eye told him stories by steering his imagination.

Did Thutmose too feel the same when he had fashioned the bust? He wondered. It would have been different for the Master Sculptor, who was also the Chief Sculptor of the Queen, and who had spent many hours alone with Nefertiti, sketching her face and sculpting it. The rumors returned to haunt him. He had heard that Thutmose and the Queen had found pleasure with each other. He found the rumors plausible for if one simply looked at Pharaoh Akhenaten, *may Aten rest his soul in peace*, and at Thutmose, it was easy to surmise why.

Quite like most other commoners, he too had only seen the white paint, the crown, and the crook and the flail, but the descriptions that he had heard of Akhenaten told him that he was tall and gangly, with a pear-shaped body and a protruding stomach that jiggled when he walked. He had no doubt that Pharaoh Akhenaten also suffered from bad breath. He had heard that when they got drunk and careless, the guards of the palace often shared salacious jokes that their Pharaoh was a woman with a stele of granite.

Thutmose, on the other hand, was built to make women dream. He was between thirty and forty, but he had a body that was as young as Sunamun's own.

The rumors, he decided, were true. Unbidden came an onslaught of images that he didn't want to see before he went to meet Thutmose, for in the last six months, he had developed a special feeling for the Queen, one that made him want to replace Thutmose in her affections and her life.

These were dangerous thoughts, especially at such a time, he cautioned himself.

Thutmose had asked him whether he would help his Queen, and he had said yes. He would do everything that he could. Not only because he loved Queen Nefertiti, but also because if she became the Pharaoh, Akhet-aten would survive, and he loved the city and his life in it.

Sunamun pulled off the coarse linen sheet that covered his bed and wrapped it around the bust. He wished he could take it along to the Royal Workshop where he was headed, but he wouldn't need it anymore, for he was going to meet the real Nefertiti.

ᘠᘠ ᘠ ᘠ ᘠ ᘠᘠ

The Royal Workshop was the place where the first casts and the reference-busts of the royals were made and approved, and so most of the year, the place wore a deserted look. It was located in an unfrequented corner of the palace compound.

Sunamun had been working in the Royal Workshop for

almost twenty days now. The limestone statue of Akhenaten stood at double his height, so Sunamun had to climb upon a stool to reach its shoulders. He hadn't left his place near the statue except for attending to his bodily functions, and for that too there was a toilet that could only be reached from the workshop.

The dim and dull interior of the Royal Workshop was a far cry from the brightly lit courtyards of Thutmose's workshop. Sunamun's new workplace was so quiet that he could hear himself breathe. Back in Thutmose's workshop it was near impossible to talk to someone who stood just a few yards away. The Royal Workshop was the stark opposite – a place where he liked to keep the lamps in the sconces burning even during the day.

While all its walls had skylights that allowed the sunlight in, almost the whole day long, the place had a cold feel to it. The stone workbenches that carried the busts sculpted by Thutmose himself, were set against three of the walls, and some of those busts that had hollows still waiting to receive the glass or the stone that would give them realistic eyeballs, stared Sunamun down, day and night.

Under the workbenches were long boxes – about three to four cubits long and a cubit high and wide. They were built in a special way allowing the box to be pulled out as a drawer. It was common practice to use such boxes to store tools and as good tools were very expensive, the boxes were usually kept locked.

Yet the boxes made Sunamun uncomfortable for a reason he could not fathom. Perhaps it was the musty smell that permeated from them that he found depressing, or their shape and size, for they reminded him of coffins.

There was a small antechamber that Thutmose used as an office, but the door opened only when Thutmose was around.

The Royal Workshop, in Sunamun's opinion, was a dark and

depressing place.

He had arrived here, happy and full of hope. He was going to work for the Queen who ruled his heart and who, he had hoped, would rule Egypt. With her face seared in his imagination, he had gone to work.

True that he was just carving a hole in the back of a statue, he was doing it for a greater purpose, and while he had his doubts about why he was set such a task, a part of him was glad for the mechanical nature of his assignment, for it allowed his mind to be free to dream.

But that was before he had met the Queen.

In his first meeting with her, he had lost his dream.

An invisible hand had positioned a chisel upon his heart. A chisel twice as big as the one he held in his hands, and used a mallet to drive the chisel in with such monstrous force that his heart had splintered into a hundred little pieces.

Two weeks had passed, two weeks of ten days each, since the day he had entered the Royal Workshop and seen the Queen.

She wore the same blue crown with the cobra wound upon it, ready to strike and protect the wearer of the crown. She also wore a pectoral that looked a little like the one she wore in the bust he had upon his table. But she had looked nothing like the Queen who had invaded his dreams. Her eyes were smaller and lighter in color, more yellow than brown. Her lips were thinner, even petulant, and she looked a lot younger than she did in the bust. Queen Nefertiti, he imagined must be almost the same age as Thutmose, and yet the Queen looked no more than twenty in person.

The pharaohs and their families had an element of divinity in them, and to sustain the impression, artists and sculptors were required to always show them at their prime. It had been different in Akhet-aten, where Pharaoh Akhenaten had approved a more realistic portrayal of the royals and the lives they led. And yet, he failed to understand why Thutmose would flesh out the corners of lips to make her look *older*, if she was this young?

The improbability of the Queen's youth had niggled at the back of his mind since he had met her. He had other questions too, but he also had known Thutmose for a long time now, and he knew that though Thutmose was apparently a devotee of Thoth, the deity of knowledge, he was also a follower of Seth, the god of chaos and evil. All Sunamun had to do was, ask one wrong question, and his own life could be in peril.

Every morning, Thutmose opened the door between the hall where Sunamun worked, and his office that he kept in the antechamber. Every morning, Thutmose came in with his cubit-scale and reviewed the progress of the hollow. He then assigned Sunamun his task for the day, handed him his food, and left. He returned in the evenings to repeat the same.

After the first few days, when he had begun to feel claustrophobic, Sunamun had asked his mentor if he could step out for a breath of fresh air.

"After you've finished," Thutmose had replied curtly, then turned and walked out into his antechamber, closing the door behind him.

Something was definitely not right. Sunamun hadn't expected to be treated with such cold indifference, especially after he had followed Thutmose's instructions so meticulously.

He shook his head and laid his chisel and hammer aside. It wasn't hot inside, but after every quarter of an hour he stopped for a short break. Sitting with his back against the wall, he reviewed his work. In the back of Akhenaten's hulking statue, he had already chiseled a hollow that was about three cubits high, and a cubit wide as well as deep. He had to contour and smoothen the edges so that the tenon of the column to which the statue would be attached, would fit the mortise snugly. Once the statue was ready, it would be wheeled out on a horse-drawn carriage and taken to the tomb, where it shall be erected in the *ka*-chamber of the deceased Pharaoh. It shall stand there for eternity, undisturbed and unchallenged – a silent witness to all that had happened and was going to happen in the Royal workshop.

Sunamun let out a long sigh. His thoughts returned to his first day in the Royal workshop. When he had first seen the Queen emerge from the antechamber with the blue crown perched upon her brow, he had immediately fallen on his knees and bowed his head.

She had asked him to rise, and he had followed her order. But then his curiosity had pushed him to glance at her face. That glance had brought his world crashing down. He had done his best to hide his shock and attempted to reason it out, unsuccessfully. The face that had infatuated him wasn't the face he saw in front of him.

Unless Thutmose was a poor sculptor, the woman in front of him wasn't the Queen.

But Thutmose was the best among the sculptors and the artists of Egypt. Sunamun recalled the story of Thutmose's rise to eminence – one that was known to every artist and sculptor in Egypt. Thutmose had once seen a bust of Queen Nefertiti and decided to sculpt another – in which she fulfilled the promise of her name, "the beautiful one has come." Then he had connived to get his work displayed to the Pharaoh and his royal wife. When the linen covering the bust was removed, the gasps from the Queen's retinue had filled the air, and the Pharaoh had asked the sculptor to step forward. When Thutmose had stepped out of the rows, the rumors said, the Queen's eyes left her own bust and stopped upon the sculptor's sculpted face.

Sunamun's shock had gradually worn off. He had made every attempt to convince himself that the Queen he met was the real Nefertiti, and the bust was merely a figment of Thutmose's imagination.

Reminded of the bust, he pined for his little room where sunlight poured in through the window that opened in the sculpting court. He missed the sounds, the smells, and the bustle of the workshop; especially the sounds, for the silence here had made him acutely aware of the life that he had left behind.

Will he ever hear them again? In the eerie silence of the Royal Workshop, memories of the banter he shared with his friend Ifeyni, the bark of Bantu the dog who the sculptors had adopted as a pup from the street, the sound of hammers and chisels and the distant hum of the grinding wheel, all flooded in to haunt him. Listening to the echoes of the monotonous sound made by his own hammer was disconcerting…and yet, silence was even worse. *Almost deathlike*, he thought and picked up his hammer again.

In the silence that wrapped the workshop, his chisel's tap-ti-tap-ti-tap was the only sound he had heard since morning. He was now learning to think of the sound as a piece of music that the gods were playing, simply to help him stay sane.

When the wooden door between the workshop and the antechamber squeaked open, he noticed it, but kept to his work. Akhenaten's huge statue hid him well and blocked his view of the door. *Must be Thutmose,* he thought and continued to work.

"How much longer is it going to take?" he heard the Queen's voice. It surprised him to hear her, but he assumed that she was speaking to Thutmose. When he didn't hear a reply, he became curious, but the fear of sidestepping the protocol kept him tethered to his spot.

It was only when he heard the soft rustle of linen and smelled the light fragrance of her perfume, he realized that the Queen had approached the statue and was now standing just next to him. He stumbled backward, trying to create space between them, and bowed.

"Your Majesty," he stuttered, "it should take three more

days."

The Queen smiled and her beauty lit up the sepulcher-like atmosphere of the workshop.

"And you think that the hollow that you have made will be sufficient for me?" she whispered, looking into his eyes. Anxious and scared, he dropped his gaze to her feet. His heart was beating faster than the wings of a hummingbird. The tension was palpable, the attraction undeniable. He had spent many nights dreaming about her, dreaming of her lips, her slender neck… the woman in front of him reflected the same intensity and exuded similar confidence. In her eyes, he saw Nefertiti; and yet, she looked a lot different and much younger.

He raised his eyes again. She was still looking at him, her soft nostrils delicately flared, her moist lips slightly parted, and her skin soft, supple, and young.

"Hold my hand and help me into it. I want to see if it fits me," her lips curled into a smile.

Before he knew, her soft hand was in his callused grip. Pushing down upon his hand gently, she raised her other arm to his shoulder and hitched herself into the recess. She stood there, about a cubit above the ground, framed in the pink of the granite, and closed her eyes.

Sunamun stood on the floor, his face a few finger-widths away from her belly. Through the diaphanous fabric, he could see her navel and smell her sweet essence. His heart hammered in his chest as he felt his desire for the Queen pulsate under his own belly. He could see the outline of her thong that she wore inside, inviting and teasing him, beckoning him, almost pulling him. He wanted to reach out and touch her, bridge the gap between them, connect with her as a man to a woman. His eyes traveled up, finding their way through the pleats of her linen robe, sliding upon her smooth skin, then rolling past her soft brown breasts tipped in bronze, then racing up her neck, they came to a stop upon her face. Her eyes were still closed and her lips parted.

But in that moment, Sunamun's worst fears were confirmed. Sweat broke upon his brow as he realized the purpose of the hollow.

The statue was going to be a secret sarcophagus.

If she was indeed Queen Nefertiti, she was planning to be buried with Akhenaten. The entire Egypt knew of the love that Pharaoh shared with Queen Nefertiti. They were the ideal couple regardless of the many wives the Pharaoh took otherwise.

His senses returned to him in a rush. He couldn't let her do that.

"Your Majesty," he whispered. His whisper came out coarse and ragged, almost dripping with passion. It shocked him and suddenly made him aware of the tension between them once again.

The Queen opened her eyes and smiled again. They were close, almost touching each other. When she reached out and pulled him to her, their breath intermingled and her perfume assailed his senses. She bent and placed her hands upon his shoulders, then lowered her face to press her mouth to his ear and whisper, "Lift me and put me down."

He followed her instruction and lifted her out of the recess. As he turned around, with her in his embrace, his eyes flicked open and his gaze fell upon the face he had forgotten about.

The handsome face of Thutmose could have been set in granite, for he had never seen it so hard. His lips were set in a line so straight that only he could've drawn it. The furrows between his brows and around his mouth looked like they were chiseled in stone, and yet the face was expressionless – his eyes were as dead as those of the statues in his workshop.

Sunamun would have dropped his burden, had he not remembered that she was the Queen. He gently put her down.

She turned to face Thutmose.

"I've tried it. It fits me well, but I don't want to run the risk of it turning out small, so let us stay with the specifications," she said, holding out her hand for Thutmose.

"Yes, Your Majesty," Thutmose replied, taking her hand and leading her away toward the antechamber.

As Sunamun watched them leave, a dark sense of foreboding filled him. Something decidedly immoral and unethical was going on, and he was right in the middle of it all.

And yet, the Pharaoh was dead, and if the rumors were true, Thutmose was very close to the Queen, and now he was very, very angry with Sunamun.

But, Sunamun closed his eyes, and thought, *it was worth it.*

ᴡᴡ 𓆓 𓆓 𓆓 ᴡᴡ

On his twentieth afternoon in the Royal Workshop, he discovered that the rumors were true.

He heard the Queen and Thutmose inside the antechamber. The sounds they made bore an eerie similarity to the ones that he had heard standing outside Thutmose's work-chamber that day, except that the woman's voice that he heard now belonged to the Queen. Even in the throes of passion, it still sounded different, contained and royal, more an expression of the pleasure that she was finding in the act, than the moans of a woman attempting to please her lover. It was oddly mesmerizing to listen to the sounds of their lovemaking, and oddly, they didn't seem to care! He wondered why they weren't concerned about their secret getting out.

And then it dawned upon him.

They didn't care, because he wasn't going to leave the Royal Workshop alive.

The sounds from the antechamber were drowned in his inner voice. The voice that beseeched him to do something and save himself, so that he could leave his mark upon the world. He would never be Pharaoh, he might never own a workshop like Thutmose did, but he knew that his art would make him famous, and that it would afford him a tomb, modest perhaps, but enough for him to make his journey into the afterlife and run free in the lush green fields of *Duat*.

He looked around frantically, searching for a way out, but he knew that if Thutmose were cunning enough to get the Queen of Egypt under him, he would have sealed every escape route.

Suddenly he did not care anymore. All he wanted to do was run away. His hostel room in Thutmose's workshop, the veiled statue of Queen Nefertiti, and even his friends, everything that he had been missing since he arrived in the Royal Workshop, suddenly lost its importance.

The sounds of lovemaking that had been trickling in from the antechamber had now been replaced with hushed whispers. He expected the door to open any moment now. Sunamun lunged to the space behind Akhenaten's statue to lean against the wall, and then he silently slid down to the ground. He closed his eyes to suggest that he was taking a nap.

A few moments later, he heard the door open. The sound of Thutmose's leather sandals tore through his eardrums. There was a time when the same sound would make him smile, for it belonged to his teacher and savior but today it filled his heart with dread.

Thutmose could have picked up any one, a stonemason or even a stone chipper, to do the job, and then killed him quietly. Instead, he chose Sunamun, the finest sculptor in Egypt – a man whose disappearance would be questioned, if not by many, at least by some. *Why did he pick me,* despaired Sunamun.

"Sunamun, are you sleeping or pretending to be asleep?"

Thutmose's question made him jump out of his skin. His eyes flickered open and tiny droplets of sweat appeared upon his brow.

"The Pharaoh's mummy is ready and sweating, waiting for his *ka* statue to be installed," added Thutmose with a smile. His smile was beguiling. Regardless of what went on in his mind, he never let it show in his face, but Sunamun knew that behind Thutmose's mask hid the cobra that used surprise as its camouflage when it struck its prey. The only time Thutmose had allowed his mask to slip was when he had witnessed the Queen in Sunamun's arms.

Sunamun sprung to his feet to stand in front of the Master Sculptor with his head bowed. Then, respectfully, he pointed at the recess in the back of the statue and said, "If you think this meets the requirement, the work is done."

Thutmose peered inside the hollow then ran a finger around its edge. Sunamun knew that the Master Sculptor was pointing out the imperfections in the edge, and he kept marking the points where Thutmose's finger paused.

"Plane these out. I'll be back in the morning," he said before leaving.

That gave Sunamun about fourteen confirmed hours of life, because in his gut he knew that Thutmose would never allow him to leave the Royal Workshop alive.

When Thutmose shut the door behind him, Sunamun slumped down to the ground, where he sat wedged between the wall and the pedestal of the hollowed Akhenaten statue.

There was nothing he could do. He sat there, devoid of all hope, doing nothing, thinking nothing. Each time he tried to think of a way out, his mind drew a blank. He wondered if shouting would be a good idea. Despite the tall windowless stonewalls that were a cubit thick, someone might hear him. And yet, the chances that the men outside didn't owe their allegiance to Thutmose or the Queen were miniscule, almost none. His only chance lay in escaping undetected. And even if he found a secret passage out, how would he leave the palace walls unseen?

I'll die here, inside this dark hall, and nobody would know, he thought frantically.

After a dark spell of despair, he saw a sliver of hope shine through a heap of unvisited memories. He remembered how the builders spoke about every royal residence being built with at least one hidden passage in and out of every chamber. With renewed hope, he got to his feet and carefully checked every cubit of the workshop. He checked the walls for a change in their texture, running fingers upon their surface, until they felt raw; he went down on his knees and tapped every stone-tile of the floor, but he couldn't detect anything. The walls and the floor were perfect. Almost like they were sculpted not built.

The realization hit him like a flint arrow shot in the center of his forehead.

The royal workshop was impermeable by design.

There   was   no   way   *out…or   in.*
After searching for hours, around the time when Ra had crossed the sky taking along with him the warmth and light, he too gave up. He collapsed against the feet of Akhenaten's statue, letting sleep gain control of his tired body.

~~~ ◊ ◊ ◊ ~~~

He awoke in the middle of the night and found the hall of the Royal Workshop bathed in the warm glow of candlelight. He had fallen asleep when the sun was setting, and he didn't remember lighting the candles. Someone was here.

Thutmose?

But Thutmose had left in the afternoon. He never returned during the night.

A sweet fragrance hung in the air – lime fresh and

feminine. It reminded him of the water lilies that bloomed in the marshes along the Nile. He looked around, checking the shadows that fell between the statues that were lined against the walls.

Memories slid back in as sleep faded. In a shock he realized that he had slept his precious time away. The realization knocked his breath out and made him fall back, but he did not fall on the ground. He fell upon a mattress.

A mattress?

He didn't remember bringing and placing his mattress next to Akhenaten's statue, and yet it was his mattress, only it was covered with a soft linen sheet.

He squeezed his eyes shut and opened them again, wondering if he was hallucinating.

Three flames burned steadily within the glass globes set upon the tallow lamps, casting soft shadows upon the tall walls, hiding the clutter upon the workbenches and outlining the sculptures, adumbrating them against the background. It was the same workshop where he had spent nearly a month, chiseling the back of a statue and converting it into a sarcophagus, little realizing that he too would be dead soon.

He cursed the day he had chanced upon the tryst between Thutmose and the mystery woman. Such escapades, in his opinion, were rather commonplace among the rich and the powerful, and it wasn't that Thutmose was a saint. Everyone, including Thutmose's wives knew of his reckless philandering. The secret that he had learned standing outside the Master Builder's work-chamber was not worth a murder.

Then why?

The answer came from an unexpected source, an unearthly vision clad in green and blue, the color of the summer Nile in the glow of the setting Sun.

"That day, when you stood outside Thutmose's work-chamber, you overheard his conversation with Nekhet, and he had no way of finding out how much you had heard," the Queen spoke from the shadows on his side. He watched her stand up and walk to him, her linen robe rippling as she moved.

The dim-light of the tallow candles didn't change the fact that the Queen didn't look like the image of her that he carried in his head, and yet he saw a hint of Nefertiti in her eyes and lips. Her face was softer and her lips decidedly thinner, and now without the blue crown, she looked like a different person.

The question that had been torturing him since he had first laid eyes on her, returned to trouble him again. *Why had Thutmose then created the original bust with a face that was so different and which made the Queen look older?*

He knew that he was on the verge of an answer. It was like he could see and feel the answer flutter in front of his eyes, but he was unable to catch it.

"What are you thinking?" the Queen demanded.

Sunamun suddenly realized that he was lying on the mattress, his *shenti* in disarray, while the Queen stood looking at him. Embarrassment flooded his face and turned it red, as he scrambled to his feet.

"Nothing at all, your Majesty," he stuttered.

The Queen pushed him back and stopped him from rising. Then slowly she lowered herself to kneel before him. The familiar feeling from the morning began filling him up, suffusing his body with an urgency that made him anxious. He found himself hoping that the Queen won't look down and discover his secret. All other concerns, including his anxiety about Thutmose's objective, began to fade into the background.

"Sunamun," the Queen said, placing her hand upon his chest, pushing him down softly. "We are here to discuss something important."

"We?" he gulped, half expecting Thutmose to step out of the shadows.

"Nekhet," the Queen called out softly.

The vision that materialized before him transported Sunamun into a different world. Even in his imagination, he couldn't have sculpted a better specimen of female beauty. She was a creation of Hathor herself, molded to be the vessel of a man's desires. Her skin was a dark lustrous mahogany and her body was molded like a goddess's. Taller than most women she was just about a palm length shorter than Sunamun himself. She wore a dress made of faience beads that fell from her shoulders and covered her hips, but left her long tapering legs bare up to her thighs. The spaces between the beads allowed him to see quick fleeting glimpses of her beautiful dark skin, the dark aureoles upon her breasts, and the mysterious triangle down below.

Sunamun felt conscious of the Queen's eyes upon him, and remembered that she had said something to him.

"Majesty, what is it that you wished to discuss," he asked, his voice trembling with a strange combination of passion and nervousness. He felt embarrassed by his rising excitement, which was nearly impossible to disguise or hide from the Queen, who sat close to him, her skin touching his.

The Queen smiled. First at him then at the Nekhet, waving her over. Nekhet followed her mistress's instructions and kneeled down in front of him.

Sunamun felt the hair on nape of his neck rise. His chest swelled with the attempt to keep his breathing regular.

"Your Majesty…" he stammered incoherently, caught between his loyalty as her subject and his desire that was on the verge of exploding. He felt the weight between his thighs grow and pulsate as blood rushed into it. His face flushed, his eyelids grew heavier, and his lips parted. The lust he felt now colored his face.

Sunamun had never seen himself in a mirror. Unmarried men seldom owned one, and so he didn't see the picture he painted for the two women in front of him. The Queen and her slave alike saw his long, lean, bronze frame with his muscles rippling from his recent chiseling effort; his aquiline nose, which was a gift from an unknown northern ancestor; his half closed eyes that conveyed his desire; his strong jawline meeting under a square chin; and his half-opened lips demanding to be kissed.

The Queen slipped down upon the rug and pulled him down to make him lie supine beside her. She touched him gently, running her fingers from his nose to his lips and chin, his neck, his chest, his stomach…and then, as he sucked his breath in, down below, making his passion rise.

The dark beauty Nekhet who had already enslaved his senses, removed the shoulder-clips of her faience dress, allowing it to slide down, letting her breasts spring free. Then she wriggled out of her dress and bent down to kiss his stele that was already ensconced in the Queen's teasing grip. His one hand found the Queen's quivering body beside him, and the other knit its fingers with Nekhet's. Through his half-closed eyes, he saw the mist of Nekhet's dark hair disperse as she straightened up and positioned herself upon him, guiding him to enter her softness, while her hand found the Queen's seat of pleasure. Engulfed in a haze of passion, he watched her as her body undulated, rose and fell, evoking fresh bursts of desire from him, and from the Queen. Later that night, Sunamun entered the royal portals and stayed there, until the Queen joined him in a cry of bliss.

"This is what I want," said the Queen afterward. Then she propped herself on her elbow and looked into his eyes.

"Do you want it too?" she asked.

It was clear to Sunamun that the Queen knew his answer, and that her question was merely rhetorical.

"Yes. Your Majesty," he replied, making her smile.

Then she told him about the box.

∿∿ 𓏏 𓏏 𓏏 ∿∿

The next morning Thutmose arrived early. He looked handsome in the new *shenti* pleated to perfection under his gem-studded waistband. The Thoth pectoral that he wore only on special occasions was around his neck, proclaiming to Sunamun that his mentor considered today an important day.

For a moment, Sunamun was transported back to the ethereal vision of last night, but he saw Thutmose in his place, first under Nekhet, then upon the Queen. He knew that last night he had taken Thutmose's place – both literally and figuratively.

"Is it ready?" Thutmose asked, laconic as ever.

Sunamun nodded. The receptacle whose purpose he now knew was sufficiently big for the task at hand.

Thutmose strode to the workbench closest to the hollowed-out statue of Akhenaten and produced a key from his pouch. Then crouching, he pushed its pins into the serrations of the lock, jerking it upward. The lock opened with a click and he pulled the huge drawer out.

Though the Queen had told him exactly what was locked in the box, still when he first laid eyes upon the mummified body in the box, he gasped. Despite his recently acquired dislike and fear for the man, he had to grudgingly accept that Thutmose had been almost as good at the priests of the necropolis in mummifying the body of Nefertiti. Her whole body lay swathed in bandages, but for some nefarious reason, Thutmose had not bandaged her face. Instead, he had painted it.

It was the face that had invaded his dreams for years. Queen Nefertiti lay in the box. Even without the tall blue crown, it would be impossible to mistake her for anyone else. Grudgingly, Sunamun admitted that Thutmose's talent exceeded his fame. Despite being desiccated by natron, her face still exuded pride and confidence. Her high cheekbones and strong jawline, and her square yet soft chin, claimed their owner as Queen Nefertiti, the beautiful one, who could have been the Pharaoh, if only her daughter Meritaten hadn't decided to take her place.

When he had first looked at the Queen's face, he had known that something was not right. She was far too young to be Nefertiti. He had not been sure because being a sculptor he knew how royal sculptors were required to bridge the gap between royalty and divinity. So when the Queen's face hadn't matched the one that he had known as Nefertiti's, he had pushed his disbelief aside. And then, there was the crown – the ultimate camouflage. The people of Egypt seldom saw the royalty close up, and when they did, the wigs and the crowns took their attention away from the royal faces. When they saw Queen Nefertiti and Pharaoh Akhenaten ride past in their chariot, all they remembered was the tall blue crown, and the graceful neck, and Princess Meritaten had inherited them both from her mother.

Could the princess be blamed for masquerading as her mother?

If he had to pin the blame on someone, he would have to seek out the *ka* of Pharaoh Akhenaten. Last night, he had received an education. He had learned that the royals lived a cursed life, and the worst of the curses that could befall a woman would be being born a princess.

He was jolted back into the present by Thutmose's gravelly voice.

"I had expected you to blanch," said Thutmose as he motioned him to lift the shoulders of the royal mummy.

For Sunamun, these had been the days of reckoning and the Royal Workshop had become his hallowed hall of learning.

On one hand, he felt repulsed by it, and on the other, he wanted to do what he had promised the Queen he would. He knew that to stay alive, he would have to choose sides, and the only side that he could choose right now, was the Queen's.

Sunamun and Thutmose together removed the body from the drawer and carried it to its sarcophagus that was formed as Akhenaten, her king, her husband, father of her six daughters and husband to two of them.

A stray glance at Akhenaten's granite face filled Sunamun with an indescribable loathing.

Where would a pharaoh stop in his mad quest of an heir?

As they went through the process of standing the mummy upright and pushing it into the recess that Sunamun had chiseled for it, another question raised its head. The answer did not matter. It would change nothing, yet it swirled into his mind.

Why would a daughter kill her mother?

Thutmose's voice brought him back once again.

"Make her stand upright. Go ahead. Hold her tight. She won't be offended by your touch," Thutmose laughed, as he prepared to fill the recess up. Sunamun was sickened by the sound of it, but he didn't let his revulsion appear on his face. He had heard the rumors that Queen Nefertiti and Thutmose were lovers, and he never doubted them.

It troubled him that Thutmose had conspired with Meritaten to *kill his own lover.* He couldn't imagine what would drive a man to commit such treason against love.

Perhaps it wasn't love that Thutmose and Nefertiti shared. Perhaps they shared just their beds.

Sunmanum climbed up into the recess at the back of Akhenaten's statue and planted his feet on either side of the royal mummy. He faced the roughly hewn granite and pushed the mummy back into the recess, making it stand while Thutmose began filling up the hole with debris.

Sunamun waited. Sweat broke out on his brow as he waited and prayed to Aten.

This could be the end of his story, his life. There was no reason why Meritaten would make good her promise to him, a junior sculptor. She might just decide to follow her original arrangement with Thutmose. If she reneged, then it would be best for him to die quickly, for it would be impossible for him to escape from the palace. Perhaps a blow on his head would help him on his way. It would be the easiest thing to do for he stood in the hole that he had dug in Akhenaten's back, with his own back exposed to Thutmose.

He shut his eyes and imagined the rays of the Sun enveloping him. Sunamun asked for forgiveness from Aten and Amun both, for he didn't know who wielded more power. He stood and waited for the blow to fall. But the blow didn't come. Not for him. Instead, he heard a scream, which was closely followed by a thud. He turned slowly.

His tall and dark paramour from last night stood behind the collapsed body of Thutmose, watching his body convulse, her features distorted with repulsion and hatred. Then her eyes looked into his, and her expression transformed.

"Will you give me hand with his body?" she asked.

He chuckled nervously, almost losing his foothold and falling down upon the crumpled form of Thutmose. He jumped down, leaving the royal mummy standing in the recess.

Yet their distraction almost took their lives, because the sword that Nekhet had driven into Thutmose's back hadn't sunk deep enough. He flopped to his side and stretched to pick up the hammer that lay among the tools that were scattered on the ground. Before Sunamun could throw himself upon Thutmose, he had already picked up the hammer. He lunged at Sunamun holding the hammer in both his hands, his face contorted with a mixture of pain and fury.

Sunamun caught the unexpected action from the corner of his eye and moved out of the path of the arc, letting Thutmose crash in the debris from the chiseling. Before Sunamun could turn to assess the situation, Nekhet had already picked up a huge chunk of granite and heaved it upon the enemy's head.

Then she waited, perspiration glistening upon her brow and shoulders. Sunamun noted that she was clad in a short linen sheath this morning, and yet, to him she looked as beautiful as she had in the night. Possibly more, for now he looked upon her without the sword of fear heavy upon his neck.

It was odd how fear and lust had worked together to heighten their pleasure and bind them together with a chain of shared guilt. Sunamun looked at the lifeless body of Thutmose and thought that despite the pain of guilt that would persist until he died, he still had a dream to follow. Thutmose's death had created a vacuum that could be filled only by someone of Sunamun's caliber.

His spirits soared once again and a smile spread upon his face.

They worked together, continuously, without stopping. First they lifted Thutmose's heavy body and made it stand against Nefertiti's, bringing them as close together in death, as they were in life. The hollow was big enough for two bodies. Only now Thutmose was accompanying Nefertiti into the afterlife and not Sunamun.

Sunamun smiled as they filled the gaps with debris. Then came the plaster to smoothen the surface and the edges of the mortise, which would receive the tenon of the pillar. Sunamun would make sure no gap remained after he was done with the plastering. It had to hold only until afternoon, because Thutmose had already scheduled the removal of the statue from the workshop. The laborers would arrive after lunch, and the statue would then be installed in the special chamber of Akhenaten's tomb – the chamber in which only the *ka* of Akhenaten, would be allowed.

And then the tomb would be sealed off.

∼∼∼ ◊ ◊ ◊ ∼∼∼

The funeral of Akhenaten was a confused affair.

His sarcophagus, which boasted of beautiful engravings of the Queen and perfect renderings of Aten's sun disks, was already established in his tomb. The tomb had an approach of about twenty steps that went downward, flanked on both sides with rooms that would be the tombs of Akenaten's favorite women – Nefertiti, his wife and Queen Consort, and Meketaten, his favorite daughter who had died giving birth to his child.

Akhenaten's mummified body had been transferred to his gold coffin, which was in turn put inside the wood coffin that had the Pharaoh's likeness painted upon it. The sides of the coffin were decorated with scenes from Pharaoh's life, same as the walls of his tomb. The priests of Aten had followed the bearers of the coffin into the tomb, descending the steps in the light of torches burning in the sconces.

The statuary was already in place, as were the objects that Pharaoh would need to continue his journey in afterlife. The *oshabtis* or the small wooden and alabaster figurines of his wives and daughters, his courtiers, his Grand Vizier and maternal uncle Ay, even one of his master sculptor Thutmose, were neatly lined up in the chamber annexed to the tomb. Then there were his clothes, his jewels, his *senet* board, his bow and a quiver full of arrows, even his reed sandals. And finally, there were the statues – these weren't the statues of Anubis and Osiris, but of the King and Queen themselves. Tall at twice the height of a normal man, they stood on the opposite sides of the sarcophagus, looking at each other, promising to be together for all eternity, under the rays of Aten engraved upon the roof of the tomb.

And yet confusion reigned. It was impossible for the priests of Aten to determine the right hymns and rituals for the first royal burial under the patronage of a single god. In the old times, they could've left their Pharaoh under the watchful gaze of Anubis, and that would've been that. Somewhere within their hearts, even the priests didn't want to prolong the burial, so after they lowered the wooden coffin into the sarcophagus, they were in a hurry to seal the tomb as soon as they could, for they didn't want to experience the wrath of the gods they had ignored.

During the ceremonies, Sunamun stood among the commoners, looking upon their new Pharaoh, wondering how many in that crowded hall actually recognized the face, for often, it wasn't the face you remembered, but the gear. The tall double-crown, the crook and the flail, the chalk-white face and the red-lips, they all came together to cast the impression of the Pharaoh, just the way the tall blue crown that sat upon the brow of the Queen told them that she was Nefertiti.

Sunamun looked around. The commoners had no idea who their Pharaoh was. They didn't care – but they trusted the royals to have chosen from their own. The commoners were there for the mortuary feast that would be held that evening. They would all gather to sing songs and pray for the Pharaoh's life to be eternal, and then they would go back to their own mundane lives – to tilling, fishing, building, to whatever they were doing the day before.

As he stood there and watched, Pharaoh Neferneferu-aten made the final offering at the mouth of the tomb, facing east, where Ra was still ascending.

Then the tomb was closed and the secrets buried.
Forever.

〰〰 𓏏 𓏏 〰〰

The morning after the burial, the announcers came again. They came beating the drums and the tambourines, shaking the rattles, and playing the harps and lutes. They came to the center of the city and raised another stele that announced that Egypt now had a new ruler, Pharaoh Neferneferuaten.

The new Pharaoh would continue to rule from Akhet-aten. Ay was still the Chief Vizier. He would be the Fan-bearer on the right side of the new Pharaoh, which meant that he would continue being the second most important man in Egypt.

Princess Meritaten, daughter and wife of Akhenaten had disappeared, but the people of Egypt could not be bothered with that minor detail. Stories were told about how Queen Nefertiti the Pharaoh's Chief Royal Wife had become the Pharaoh and had the blessings of Aten to be the Pharaoh and rule upon Egypt as Neferneferuaten.

That evening, one of the two men who knew the whole truth, slipped beside the new Pharaoh in the royal bed. That morning he had been awarded the title, The Chief Sculptor of Pharaoh Neferneferuaten.

According to the rumors, Thutmose, his predecessor in the royal bed and in position, had left Akhet-aten and gone away to Thebes. He was never seen again, but the Workshop was in business again, for the construction of Pharaoh Neferneferuaten's tomb had already begun, and the statues had to be made quickly.

The Workshop was now called Sunamun's Workshop.

〰 𓏢 𓏢 𓏢 〰

Ay stood near the window of Nefertiti's room and looked out. Nobody had stood in this window for almost six months now. It had belonged to the girl child that his wife had adopted thirty-five years ago.

Nearly forty years ago, when Ay was a young man, and when his sister Tiye had married Amenhotep, third of that name, he had begun planning his destiny. He had brought about the match between his nephew Akhenaten and Nefertiti. All that the sickly gangling goat had to do was produce a boy with Nefertiti, and everything would have fallen in place.

But he had failed. Not once or twice, but six times, they had produced daughter after daughter, until Ay's own hair had turned gray. Ay had waited patiently for a grandson to arrive, for in the event of Akhenaten's untimely death, a grandson would have made him the most powerful man in Egypt.

A wisp of a song floated to him from across the river.
You are my Ka, my Amun, my Ra…

Ay ignored the song. He had plans to make, strategies to build – and if things worked out for him, he would have a nation to rule.

He had done everything to make the wheels of fortune turn for him. He had even supported the mad king when he had come up with the idea of a single god. He had stood by Akhenaten's side for sixteen long years, guiding him, helping him, telling him how to rule. All he had asked for was that Akhenaten declared him, Ay, as his heir. But that foul smelling androgynous clod had made Nefertiti his coregent, so that she may rule Egypt after him.

Ay had accepted that too. He was sickened by the thought that a mere woman of unknown antecedents would wear the crown and rule the great land of Egypt, but he had accepted it.

She wouldn't know how to rule, he had thought, and I will hold the power.

But she knew it all, except that she didn't know that her knowledge and ability would become her death.

Knowledge, he smiled, was the most powerful weapon that a man could wield. He knew about Nefertiti and Thutmose, and he knew Thutmose better than Nefertiti did. Ay understood and appreciated the power of greed and lust, and he had the ability to make men and women dance to the tunes of these two emotions.

Ay looked out of the window and saw the farmer and his wife. Small, insignificant figures on the horizon.

The next few lines that the farmer's wife sang made him smile.

When you touch me, I come alive,
You kiss me and make me fertile,
Without you, I am a dry desert,
Your touch makes me Kemet.
You are my Ka, my Amun, my Ra…

He had won the game. He had established Meritaten as Pharaoh Neferneferuaten, because he understood desire and hatred.

Desire enslaved women the same it enslaved men. Deep within, women hated the experience of lying under a bag of wrinkled skin and being kissed by a mouth full of rotting teeth. When a man took a woman by force and against her wishes, despite all the bonds that may tie her to him, the idea of carrying the seed of such a man in her womb often turned the woman into a dormant volcano of hatred.

Ay had seen that hatred smoldering in the eyes of Meritaten when her younger sister Mekaten had died trying to give birth to their father's child, and he knew of the revulsion Meritaten had felt when she had thrown up after her first night as her father's bride.

After the first night that she had spent with Thutmose, Mertitaten had given Aye her ear.

He wished Nefertiti had too. If she had, neither she nor Thutmose would be dead.

Outside the window, across the Nile, he saw the farmer and his wife leave. His hand was wrapped around her shoulder – to love and protect her.

Ay had his own love to nourish.

He would let the new Pharaoh celebrate with the young handsome sculptor in her bed, while he would rule Egypt, because Ay knew the truth that others did not.

The Pharaoh never ruled. The man who had the Pharaoh's ear, did.

᠊ᠠᠠᠠ 𓏏 𓏏 𓏏 ᠊ᠠᠠᠠ

Historical Notes:

Akhet-aten was the capital of Egypt under the rule of Akhenaten. Akhenaten, who was called the heretic king for proposing Aten as the sole god, had first ruled from Thebes but later moved his capital to Akhet-aten, now known as Amarna.

Nefertiti, the most famous face that looks at us across time, is said to have vanished from the historical records completely after the 16th regnal year of the heretic king Akhenaten who died in the 17th year of his reign.

It is impossible to tell who reigned after Akhenaten and before Tutankhaten (who later changed his name to Tutankhamun.) However, two names, Neferneferuaten and Smenkkhare, have puzzled historians, because they appear to belong to a woman Pharaoh. Historians theorize about this Pharaoh being either Nefertiti or Meritaten, but there are no clear indications of her being either.

The Nefertiti Bust is a painted stucco-coated limestone sculpture of Nefertiti's head. It is believed that Thutmose had sculpted it during Akhenaten's rule. It was found in his workshop in Amarna, Egypt.

Nefertiti's bust has one of its eyes missing, and experts are of the opinion that the left eye of the bust, for an unknown reason, was never completed.

Meritaten and Mekaten were the first and second daughters of Akhenaten and Nefertiti. Pharaoh Akhenaten had taken these two princesses as his wives, and attempted to sire a male heir through them. Mekaten had died trying to produce Akhenaten's child.

Ay was the brother of Akhenaten's mother, and hence, his maternal uncle. It is also conjectured that he may have been Nefertiti's father, as his wife was Nefertiti's wet-nurse.

When Tutankhaten, his maternal grandson ascended the throne at the age of eight, Ay became his regent.

Story Four

THE SAVIOR OF EDFU

~ | First Intermediate Period | ~

THE SAVIOR OF EDFU

Ankhtifi was sailing north, back to Nekhen, his nome and home. Standing upon the deck of his barge, he turned to look back at Edfu receding into the horizon and felt the warm summer breeze caress his face. The nome of Edfu now had a new nomarch who would govern it not just with cunning and intellect but with care and love, of this he was sure. Ankhtifi's own destiny lay north, and that was where he would go. His work in Edfu was done – the hand of fate had moved over his destiny and the destiny of those in Edfu, and was sure that it was neither to smite nor to smother, but to rekindle happiness and trust.

And yet, he sighed, *I, Ankhtifi, The Prince, Count, Royal Seal-bearer, Sole Companion, Lector-priest, General, Chief of scouts, Chief of foreign regions, the one who had been brought to Edfu to rejuvenate it, couldn't foresee it?*

And yet, he reflected, *I, Ankhtifi, who finds the solution where it is lacking, a leader of the land through active conduct, a man strong in speech and collected in thought, failed to see how this would end?*

~~~ 𓃀 𓃀 𓃀 ~~~

"It will soon be dark," Yuya looked at the darkening silhouettes of the cliffs that towered over, and observed. With a missing front tooth and a scar that angrily rose from the bridge of his nose and flew across his forehead, Yuya looked his part. He was Meret's deputy and the man in-charge, and it was his responsibility to keep the slaves in line. With just six armed guards, three of whom had a rather questionable background, he had to be extra cautious. The cargo was precious, not only because they were bringing in expensive slaves from across the Mediterranean, but also because Meret, the most resourceful trader in Egypt, was on a mission. He hadn't divulged the details of the mission to Yuya, but Yuya had surmised that it had something to do with Edfu.

Meret, the portly middle-aged trader who had recently developed an inexplicable love for upper-garments, noted Yuya's observation and nodded. He sported a sparse mustache that struggled to cover his upper lip and a sparser beard, which begged to be ignored in view of his substantial jowls that harked for attention. His thin linen shirt clung to his torso like a second, rather wet skin, but he was oblivious of any discomfort, including his raw bottom. Sitting astride a donkey the whole day wasn't easy but Meret liked to be in control and riding in a palanquin made it impossible to keep an eye on everyone and everything. He often wondered how some other traders managed their business from behind the curtains of a litter.

"There's a traveler's well coming up and it would be a nice place to break for the night," Yuya informed him before barking out orders to the vanguard and falling back to ensure that everyone toed the line.

All the members in the caravan knew what they had to do. Most of them had traveled together from the port of Tanis at the mouth of the delta, and had been together for more than three months now.

The women quickly dug little holes in the ground and brought out the adobe bricks for their makeshift stoves. Some started the fires; a few began kneading the millet flour with camel milk, while others cleaned the fish, setting them up on the sticks to grill.

The men busied themselves with pitching the tents, feeding the donkeys and massaging their limbs to prepare them for the long trot the next day.

The slave girls sat in a tight huddle, whispering and sharing their apprehensions as they waited to be fed.

It wasn't long before the desert air began to cool down. The rich aroma of *dhurra* bread being baked and dipped into butter and the river-fish being grilled on the fires, hung low in the air, and began tickling and whetting the hunger of the travelers.

The men in the caravan were sharing rambunctious stories and cracking salacious jokes, hoping to find a companion to slumber with for the night, when Meret found his way around the tents and the fires to find the group of slaves he was looking for. They were a small group intended for a special viewing by the nomarch of Edfu, Khuy, who was known for his voracious appetite of almost everything. His collection of jewels could compete with Pharaoh's; his kitchen employed cooks from lands even Meret hadn't visited; and his harem was home to more than a hundred exotic beauties, some from lands beyond the eastern shores.

As he approached, one of the girls stood up and walked out of the huddle. Tall and slim, she was of light-brown complexion with intelligent eyes. She had joined the caravan in Nekhen. Meret knew that she wasn't the prettiest of the lot. And yet, she was the one he had intended to meet.

She came closer and curtsied.

"Are you anxious?" he enquired.

"A little, but I can handle it," she replied, tilting her head coquettishly. He noticed that the gesture didn't suit her lanky frame and her plain face, but he didn't want to say anything to demoralize her.

"We'll be reaching Edfu by noon tomorrow. Be prepared," he looked into her eyes. She looked back.

Definitely not a slave, he thought.

The girl returned to the group, her shapeless frame and awkward gait making him wonder whether she was indeed a woman.

Perhaps a eunuch.

As he meandered through his camp, he reflected upon his meeting with Ankhtifi, the nomarch of Nekhen. The man was a giant of sorts. These were terrible times. Egypt was in turmoil. Lower Egypt now had its own Pharaoh who had claimed Henen-nesut as the capital. The Theban nomarch Mentuhotep had declared himself Pharaoh of Upper Egypt. The declaration, however, wasn't worth the price of the papyrus it was written on, because Mentuhotep's control didn't extend beyond Thebes. He had attempted to bring Nekhen, the nome to the south of Thebes, under his rule, but Ankhtifi was a shrewd statesman who not only had the support of the people of Nekhen, but also of Henen-nesut.

It was indeed a difficult period for Egypt and Egyptians, for the lack of a central authority had brazened the nomarchs, the officials, and even the priests. The government officials were taking corruption to new heights, the priesthood was exercising its influence over royalty and commoners alike, the gods appeared to be deserting Egypt, and the nomarchs had turned into competitors, or worse, into enemies. The population of Egypt was suffering; the traders were being taxed, double-taxed, and yet looted, because the roads had turned unsafe. It was only in the nome of Nekhen in Upper Egypt where one could still experience the richness of Egyptian culture, and the credit of it went to Ankhtifi.

Two nights ago, Meret had dined with Ankhtifi, a rare and unexpected honor. Upon meeting Ankhtifi, he realized why the man had been able to keep his nome untouched and untainted by the plague of uncertainty that was sweeping across Egypt. He realized how Ankhtifi's ideas could change the fortunes of Egypt. In his forty-nine years, Meret had met many nomarchs and lords. He had even had the good fortune of kneeling in front of both the pharaohs, and yet Ankhtifi was unlike anyone else. He was a strange concoction of pride, intellect, ruthlessness, and compassion.

If anyone could change the destiny of Egypt, Ankhtifi could. And Meret, now his friend for life, would stand by him.

〰 𓏤 𓏤 𓏤 〰

The next day, just before noon, Meret's caravan entered Edfu. Around the same time, a bell rang in the House of Khuy.

The bell's origins dated back to the time of Khuy's great grandfather and it could be rung from the guardroom in the city-center. In the guardroom was a lever that was connected through ropes and pulleys to the huge brass bell that hung in the courtyard of the House of Khuy. Anyone who wanted to make a complaint directly to the nomarch could go to the guardroom and toll the bell by pulling the lever.

Nowadays, the bell rang a lot more frequently. Sometimes a dozen times in a day. Khuy had been thinking of having it dismantled, but through her will and wile Ashayt had convinced him to leave it alone. Without the bell to warn her, she wouldn't have known anything to be amiss in Edfu, for inside the House everything was always fine.

From her window in the kitchen, Ashayt could see the bell being tolled. The rope that was tied to the gong of the bell alternated between going taut and slack, making Ashayt imagine the unseen hand that was tolling it. It wasn't easy to toll the bell. She had heard from the kitchen staff that the guards had to be bribed to access the bell, and when she had complained to Khuy about it, he had laughed it off.

"If I could, I'd bribe them too, so that they'd stop that useless riffraff from tolling that infernal bell," he had replied, tossing a grape into his mouth.

Though Ashayt was the principal wife of Khuy, and she had no reason to leave her own chambers and come down to the kitchen where the slaves worked, she often did. She liked being in the kitchen. It had more life in it than the whole house had, for there she could meet the grocers, the milkmen, the fishwives, the vegetable-sellers, and watch the kitchen staff as they bustled around trying to ensure that everything was perfect for Governor Khuy. The kitchen staff woke up before dawn, while Khuy, spent and tired after his nocturnal orgies, slept until afternoon. This was a boon for the kitchen staff as they had the entire morning to themselves. They laughed and joked, as they prepared Khuy's first meal of the day, and Ashayt loved watching them, because they reminded her that happiness wasn't a myth.

But then there was the matter of the bell.

She knew what was wrong. The people of Edfu were suffering. The rot of corruption had seeped in so deep that it had become impossible for an honest man to conduct business without bribing the officials, and the bribes were so high that those who employed others for work, found it difficult to pay the wages. So the wages of the working class had dropped below subsistence level, and the hungry masses were now on the verge of a revolt. Naturally, the priests thrived on this despondency, and made promises to invoke one god or the other, to help anyone who would pay them for their service, so the rich and the poor alike were flocking around these dishonest priests.

The bell tolled again.

Ashayt rose to leave. Perhaps the gods had willed Edfu into oblivion, and now there was no other way left, except to invoke the gods themselves.

She was about to leave for her chambers when the scullery maid came running to her. Down here in the kitchen, they all knew Ashayt and loved her.

"Lady Ashayt," the maid was nearly incoherent as she bubbled with excitement. "The caravan is here, and they'll be coming to the House to show their wares tonight."

Her words lifted the great weight of pessimism off Ashayt's shoulders. She smiled and waved the maid away to her dishes.

The caravan was a beacon of light in their otherwise hopeless lives. It brought new people into the household. True that they were all slaves, but their arrival changed the way people interacted with one another. New relationships were formed, love blossomed, anger and jealousy were born – the caravan brought stories and rejuvenated their tired and unhappy world.

The bell tolled again… and again.

The bell was challenging her. It was asking her to stop it from tolling if she could. She would, if only she could.

Perhaps the gods will turn kind and show her the path. Among all in Edfu, she was the only one who had the will, the strength, and the courage to accomplish it. The people didn't have the strength, Khuy had neither the will nor the courage, and so it fell upon her.

She turned to look at the bell. It had just gone still.

She felt like the bell had grown eyes and they were riveted to hers telling her that the challenge was real. She tilted her head a little and looked straight into the eyes of the bell she was seeing.

"I accept your challenge," she muttered under her breath. Then she straightened her shoulders and turned away from her adversary, the bell that had been torturing her ever since she had set foot in Edfu.

The night was important. Meret's caravan came only once a year, and tonight she had to buy a slave.

She had to stop the tolling bell.

ᗰᗰ 𝄆 𝄆 𝄆 ᗰᗰ

When the sun set upon the Nile coloring it a mysterious deep mauve, the gates of the House of Khuy opened to admit Meret and Yuya. Behind them appeared Meret's own slaves from the land of Nubia and beyond, their dark skin glistening as their muscles rippled under the weight of the treasures they were carrying. A dozen veiled women wearing long skirts followed the treasure bearers – they had chains connecting them to one another, a simple device to give them some room to maneuver without giving them an opportunity to run away. In the rear were two armed guards, who were stopped outside the House of Khuy.

They were received in the richly carpeted audience hall that had a throne-like seat in the front row. There was another smaller chair neither as ornate nor as big as the other. A fool could have guessed that the throne was meant for Khuy and the smaller chair for his brother Simonthu.

Behind the throne and the chair, carpets were laid out for the rest of Khuy's household. Meret would have loved to have some children in his audience for they greatly influenced the buying decisions of their parents, always to Meret's advantage.

Khuy, however, was known to keep children away from such displays. So the first ones to appear in the audience hall were the concubines and the maids. They settled down upon the carpets that were laid behind the throne and filled the air with their low murmurs.

Meret busied himself preparing the display. The bearers had unburdened themselves and were now unrolling the carpets while Meret opened the chests one by one, bringing out the silverware from Syria and Turkey, and boxes of *bhang* that he had bought from a ship that had sailed from India. Then he brought out the jewelry – mostly made of faience beads but some with precious gems mostly turquoise, lapis lazuli, amethyst, and malachite. Egyptians loved blues and greens for these were the colors of life – the blue of the sky and the green of the Nile. He hoped that at least a few of Khuy's famed hundred wives would be joining them.

The slaves were receiving their final instructions from Yuya. He looked rather comical attempting to act feminine, which reminded him of that tall woman who didn't appear to be a slave and who had joined his caravan in Nekhen. Despite the veil, it wasn't difficult to identify her. She stood taller than the rest – almost as tall as Yuya himself. *She was the key*, he thought. Meret had no inkling about what she was expected to do, but he was told that she was the most important merchandise in his cargo, and that no harm should come to her. He had already been compensated for bringing her here, so it didn't matter how much the House of Khuy was willing to pay for her – Meret would have happily given her away.

He watched as the slave girls lifted their veils partially to display their bellies, bosoms, and lips, and moved their hips slowly and seductively. Just a month ago, they wouldn't have done any of it, but after their long and eventful journey, all they wanted was to find a sliver of permanence, and being bought by a nomarch was one of the best things that could happen to them.

"Lord Khuy, Governor of Edfu, and his brother Lord Simonthu are ready to view your wares now," the crier announced the arrival of their host.

Meret and Yuya motioned the others to stand back, while they stood in front with their heads bowed. This was Meret's ninth visit to Edfu. He had been in the presence of Khuy eight times before tonight, and he had witnessed the gradual expansion of Khuy's body.

"Meret, my old friend! Welcome to Edfu once again. Do you know how eagerly we all await your annual visit here?" Khuy asked. Meret noticed, not without some degree of repulsion that Khuy had lost three of his front teeth and his breath smelled rotten, yet he forced a smile as he greeted the nomarch politely.

"My Lord, I am grateful for your patronage," he said, hoping that he didn't sound mendacious and that his deep dislike for the man hadn't seeped into his voice.

Khuy smiled and gestured him to start.

First the carpets were unrolled. The woolen carpets were works of art. They weren't meant for the floor, but for the walls as they covered the ugly white limestone that was used in most of the Egyptian buildings. As they were unrolled, ethereal pictures of an imaginary paradise appeared. Rivers, nymphs, birds, swans, trees, and flowers – none like the ones that they saw in Egypt. In moments, the floor had transformed into a beautiful landscape. Gasps went up from the audience, making Meret look up and scan their faces. They were all mesmerized. Behind Khuy and his brother, about two score wives belonging to both the brothers had trailed in. Most of them were middle-aged and fat, and from what he had heard, many had spent just a single night in their husband's bed, for the nights of the brothers mostly belonged to the slaves and the prostitutes.

His eyes returned to Khuy and then to his brother. Khuy was complacent. The carpets and their beauty didn't interest him, but his brother, the halfwit, was enthused by the wild display of figures and colors in front of him. He had drawn one leg up and tucked it under his buttocks. He sat there with his eyes popping out from under his arched brows, and his index finger in his mouth. While he looked like a jester, it was clear that he wasn't as fond of food as his brother, and that his appetite for art still wasn't jaded.

Meret turned his attention to the brother. It was rumored that Khuy never denied any request of his brother, and Meret himself had witnessed this on more than one occasion in the past.

"My Lord Simonthu, may I present the carpets for your evaluation? I think that the one with those five nymphs bathing in the river of paradise would look lovely on the wall of your bedchamber."

Lord Simonthu acknowledged his attention by making a gurgling sound and stomping his foot on the floor.

"Meret, it appears that Lord Simonthu approves of this carpet, so we will buy it. What else do you have for us?"

For the next watch until the night fell and the only light in the chambers came from the tallow lamps that burned bright in each sconce, Meret displayed his wares to the brothers and their wives. The perfumes from the east, the jewels from the north and across the sea, the softest linen in the most beautiful greens and blues, the rich silk in a wide range of colors varying from crimson to purple and midnight blue, the painted and glazed pottery with images of paradise, and the game-boards made of ivory and ebony tiles set in gold. The wives wanted to see it all, but Khuy was impatient. That he had been sipping wine all through the display didn't help his mood.

"Meret, be done with the trinkets. The wives can squabble over it for a whole week, and not make up their minds. Did you bring your donkeys all this way only to ferry these baubles?" Khuy sneered.

Meret quickly got the area cleared. It was now Yuya's turn to show his merchandise to its best advantage. The slave-show was usually deferred until the sun had set, because the warm glow and the softening light of the candles often hid the imperfections of the skin and features, and transformed every woman into a beauty.

So while Meret receded in the background to review his depressingly short list of orders, Yuya started the slave show. The women were ready. Yuya had tutored them well. One after the other, they flung their robes aside and sashayed up to the brothers, their faces still veiled with muslin so thin that it was almost non-existent. They wore little cups woven from faience beads to cover the aureoles of their breasts and when they turned, their skirts wrapped around their thighs in soft liquid movements. Meret watched the expressions of the brothers carefully. Khuy's lusty gaze was riveted to the lithe ebony frame of the Nubian whom Meret had bought from a southern merchant for two expensive Persian rugs. His half-wit brother's eyes were still jumping from one woman to another.

He would never make up his mind, Meret thought.

"My Lord," he curtsied low in front of the brother. "Who do you like the best?"

The troll's tongue darted out, sprinkling Meret with his saliva, who tightened his facial muscles to stop his revulsion from showing upon his features. With his eyes popping out, Khuy's brother pointed his finger at the plump Egyptian who Meret had procured from Memphis.

"She...ee..." he drawled, but then his eyes flitted to the slim young girl behind her, who caught his glance, and tried to hide in the shadows.

"Yes, my Lord," Meret prodded, hoping that he won't ask for the young one. From what he had heard about the halfwit, he was double the monster his brother was, and the girl was too young.

"My Lord, Nija here learned her craft in the temple of Bes," he ventured, tapping the Egyptian woman's shoulder.

On his cue, the well-endowed Egyptian unhooked her skirt and turned to display her generous buttocks to them. Within moments, the brothers had made up their mind.

And yet, another slave must be sold tonight, Meret thought frantically, wondering how he could strike the most important deal of the night. Neither Khuy nor his brother had spared the tall one another glance.

Oblivious to Meret's dilemma, Yuya motioned the two selected girls to stand aside and others to fall back.

"There's another…" Meret began, his voice cracking with nervousness, when he saw Lady Ashayt stand up. Before tonight, he had only seen her once, and that was six years ago. Until now, he hadn't noticed her, mainly because he hadn't expected to see her again. He remembered from that last visit that she hadn't bought anything.

"My Lord," she addressed Khuy, "will it meet your approval if I too chose a slave?"

Khuy laughed.

"Ashayt? You want a woman too? Go ahead and choose, but send her to us tomorrow. Tonight we won't have the time to sample your merchandise," he snickered.

Meret watched their exchange with interest. Ashayt's lovely face didn't register any emotion – neither of anger, nor of annoyance. She turned to Meret and smiled.

For a moment Meret forgot to breathe. He had heard that there was a time when poems were written and songs were composed about her beauty in the southern nomes. Now looking at her, he knew why. He retraced his step and bowed to her. Then he followed her as she strode out to the line of women that stood against the wall.

She assessed the women, turning their heads to face her, until she reached the tall one. A gold scarab with faience beads set in its wings awkwardly sat glinting upon her prominent collarbone. Her light gray eyes had a piercing gaze that could stop a man dead in his tracks, and she stood almost a head taller than Ashayt.

"I'll take her," she pointed at the tall one, who stepped out of the line and fell behind Ashayt.

Khuy who had been watching it silently, broke into peals of laughter as she walked back with her new slave in tow.

"While I can't imagine what you'd want to do with her, don't send her to our chambers, tomorrow night or any other night," he shouted.

"Don't send, don't send," mimicked the halfwit, as a relieved Meret waited for Khuy to put the Governor's seal of approval upon the list of articles he had sold tonight. The girls they had chosen had found their places at the feet of the nomarch and his brother.

Meret's work here was done. Tomorrow he would get paid and leave for Nekhen.

~~~ 𓂋 𓂋 𓂋 ~~~

As night fell over the limestone building that housed the nomarch's residence and office, lamps were snuffed and torches quenched in nearly all the chambers, except in those that belonged to Khuy and his family.

Ashayt sat in front of her *ankh*-table, while Myla, her new acquisition, groomed her hair with a shell-comb.

Ashayt looked at her reflection in the polished bronze of the mirror. She was aging, and while strands of silver were beginning to appear in her otherwise dark hair, her skin was still supple and the fine lines around her mouth and eyes were impossible to see unless one looked closely. Her eyes, she was told often, were beautiful. Her upper eyelids were lined with thick eyelashes that canopied over her deep brown eyes, hiding them partially, lending her an aura of mystery. Her nose was straight but its tip though small was soft and round, like a child's, and it made her look younger than her years; yet the childlike quality of her face was offset beautifully by her sensual lips that curved ever so slightly at the corners.

Sitting in front of the mirror, surrounded by the floral fragrances exuded by the candles, Ashayt was transferred to the days before she had wedded Khuy. Those were beautiful days, when she dreamed of a life that would be filled with love. She was born in the house of Kare, the richest merchant in Nekhen. It was when she had turned fifteen that her eyes had first fallen upon the handsome young man who had come to meet her father one afternoon. She had sat next to her father during lunch, hoping that her father's handsome guest would look at her in a special way, but he hadn't spared her a glance.

When she learned that he had felt the same way about her, a year had passed and she had become the wife of Khuy. The rage that she had felt then, the impotent anger that sloshed in her gut when she had discovered the monster that Khuy was – it was still alive, and for all her efforts, her face must have reflected it, because she suddenly realized that Myla had stopped combing her hair, and she was watching her face in the mirror with a look of grave concern.

Ashayt turned and looked at Myla.

"Are you prepared?" she asked.

Myla nodded.

"Good. Let us go then," whispered Ashayt, motioning Myla to pick up the lamp that stood on her *ankh*-table.

They walked together through the narrow aisle, an

unlikely pair but with the closeness of sisters, for their purpose bound them in a bond stronger than that of blood. They kept close, their bodies touching and exchanging warmth and comfort.

At the end of what felt like a very long walk; they stopped in front of a wooden door. Ashayt cracked it open. She had expected the sounds she heard. The lusty whispers of the slave girls feigning pleasure, the guttural laughter of Khuy, and the senseless giggles of the idiot who mimicked his doting brother's every act, filled the air around them.

They tiptoed into the chamber, ignoring the smell of sweat, wine, and sex that permeated the atmosphere. Standing in the shadows, they watched the scene that was lit up before them. Khuy lay supine on the bed. The Nubian sat between his legs, massaging his phallus, attempting to make it rise, but Khuy was too drunk to feel any of it. Perhaps he found her touch somewhat ticklish, because her effort was punctuated by his laughter. At once, Ashayt knew that her husband was more drunk than usual. His brother, the halfwit, was attending to the torture of the Egyptian woman, pinching, hitting, and slapping her, making her squeal and scream, while he giggled endlessly.

Ashayt and Myla slipped inside. The girls weren't expecting them, but they knew Myla well from the long trip along the Nile, and when she gestured them to step aside and leave the room, they understood and withdrew into the same dark gully that Ashayt and Myla had emerged from, softly closing the door behind them.

The halfwit watched them with interest, his tongue sticking out of the side of his mouth, when he suddenly realized that his prize was gone. He opened his mouth to scream. Myla had however anticipated his action, so before he could scream, she took him in her arms, and began kissing him. The poor brute had never been embraced before, and he didn't know what to make of it, except making gurgling noises as he buried his head between her breasts.

Ashayt went to work immediately taking over from where the Nubian had left over. The unguent was strong and before long, it would begin to take effect. At first, it would soothe, then it would burn, and finally it would paralyze. Ashayt focused on his instruments of torture – first his member, then his teeth and tongue, and finally his hands. The poison would work quickly, but she'd still have time to enjoy watching him writhing in pain.

Sitting beside her husband, watching his eyes fly open as he gasped for breath, she reached out for the gold scarab pendant, snapped it shut, and passed it back to Myla.

᎙᎙᎙ 𓏲 𓏲 𓏲 ᎙᎙᎙

Ankhtifi got the news from Meret, who had sent his runner with a small wooden box that contained a beautiful scarab, its wings decorated with faience beads set in gold. He held it between his fingers and thumb and flipped it open. The tiny chamber inside was empty.

The deed was done.

The people of Edfu were saved, because Ankhtifi had fulfilled his promise to Ashayt. He closed his eyes and allowed himself the luxury of imagining how things would be now. Ashayt would have already announced him as the Savior to the people of Edfu. When his barge would sail into Edfu, both the banks would be lined with crowds that would sing praises of him. They would wave palm fronds and silk banners to welcome him to Edfu. They would engrave reliefs that would tell stories of how Ankhtifi saved Edfu. Of course, the tactical details would forever remain buried, but then the gullible commoners should only be too glad to believe that the gods had heard their prayers. They would also as readily believe that

Ankhtifi's arrival right at the time when their nome needed him the most, was due to divine intervention.

He looked at the empty shell of the gold scarab once again, and thought that she had touched it too. He picked it up, brought it to his nose and sniffed. The smell was almost gone. If the poison were as effective as Meret had promised, Khuy wouldn't have suffered long. It came from the depths of the mystical seas of the east, and if the stories were true, a hundred men could be killed by just a few drops – the unguent required that it wasn't touched by bare hands, and so it was transported in a little leather pouch that was made of many layers of leather; and he hoped that Ashayt hadn't taken it upon herself to administer it to Khuy.

The thought twisted his gut into a knot of blinding jealousy. She was not his. If only he had sensed the evil intentions of Lord Kare, he would have given him twice the land that Khuy did, in exchange of his marriage with Ashayt.

He hadn't. He had waited, for Ashayt was still young, and he thought there was time. Unfortunately for both, before he could confess his love to her, she was married to Khuy. He had tried to avoid thinking about her. Later, in time, he too had married. His four marriages were strategic devices, designed to help him further his career, but the thorn of his first love had remained embedded in his heart, giving him pain yet keeping him alive, for everything else in his life had become a rut and everyone a fixture – never evoking emotions that the thorn made him experience.

So when seventeen years later, he had received her message, he found it both incredible and exhilarating. The message was simple and direct. "When Sun touches its reflection in the Nile, meet me at the Lodge of Hapi."

The little scarab box pendant in which the message was delivered was the one he had sent his failed love-message in. She had kept it all those years, and she had trusted him to remember.

He had gone for the rendezvous, half expecting it to be a ploy, but riding on the hope that he was right.

When he had reached the quay of the Lodge of Hapi that was known throughout the Upper Egypt for keeping secrets, and he was escorted to the lady's chambers, he could hear his own heart thumping against his ribs.

A maid whose face he couldn't recall had admitted him into the antechamber. Standing there, through the translucent muslin curtain that separated the living chamber from the antechamber, he saw her silhouette. She stood against the railing of the *baradari* that allowed the sweet Nile breeze in.

The maid went out, closing the door of the antechamber behind her. He knew that this was his last chance to turn and follow the maid out. It could be Ashayt or it could be a trap. He chose to stay. Softly lifting the muslin curtain, he walked out into the *baradari*.

"Ashayt," he called her name.

She turned and looked into his eyes. Then they didn't talk for a very long time. The Sun had kissed its reflection in Nile when he had entered the lodge; when they finally broke their embrace long enough to talk, the moon was already high in the sky.

"You are more beautiful than ever," he said, gently pushing the lock of hair away from her forehead.

"I'm older too," she replied.

"And wiser?" he queried.

"Yes, but I won't wish such wisdom upon my enemies," she mused, turning her face away, but Ankhtifi had seen the glint of a tear in her eye, so he softly turned her face back to look into her eyes.

"You mean upon Khuy?"

She couldn't stop her tears from rolling down, so she hid her face in his chest and sobbed. Even in the dull light of the single candle that they had left burning, he could see the weals on her back. Some had healed long ago, others looked fresh.

"He hits you?" He suddenly lost his composure. She was a noblewoman, the wife of a nomarch, and she had rights. In those days of Egypt's glory, when the nome governors were Pharoah's representatives, and not self-proclaimed nome rulers, this would have been impossible. And yet, these were some of the blackest decades in the history of Egypt – the Pharaoh was a weak ruler whose power reduced with each step one took away from Thebes, and the nome governors considered themselves kings. He had even heard that some nome governors had amended the rulebook to include their own rules and remove the ones that didn't serve their interests.

Her voice brought him back to her. She had stopped sobbing and was now looking at him.

"Yes, he hits me. But that's not the worst of him. Inside the nome-palace, we are fed and clothed. He is an alcoholic and a pervert and so is his brother…"

"His brother, the halfwit?" Ankhtifi interjected. He had seen Khuy's brother once, some twenty years ago, when he was six. He found it difficult to imagine a six-year-old with no control over his movements or thoughts, as a drunk pervert.

"They do everything together. They share their food, their women, even their bedchamber! The only person Khuy loves other than himself is Simonthu," Ashayt said, pulling herself up and turning to sit in front of him.

Her proximity distracted him, and he reached out to stroke her thigh. She gently pushed his hand away.

He knew that the moment of truth was about to arrive now, and he also had an intuition of what that truth might be, so when she reached out to hold his hand and asked him, he wasn't surprised.

He had left the lodge the next morning a new man - a

man filled with purpose and determination; a man who still had a dream. Once Ashayt and Edfu were free, both would become his.

The empty scarab shell was proof that both were now free.

He removed his gold chain from his neck and slipped the pendant on it.

"Get my barge ready to sail. We are going to Edfu," he announced as he ran up the steps to his work-chamber.

He was going to Edfu, where he would meet her again and when they'd be together alone, he would slip the chain around her neck, and their story would come to an end that they both desired and deserved. She would then be his favorite wife, and he would never hurt her. Nor would he ever marry again, and then he would make her a chamber in his tomb, where she would follow him into the afterlife, so that they may be together forever.

ᗰᗰᗰ 𓏤 𓏤 𓏤 ᗰᗰᗰ

When Ankhtifi's barge pulled into Edfu, he came to the deck to watch the crowds that he was expecting. He had sent a faster ship to Edfu with the news that he would be reaching there to pay his respects to Edfu's departed nomarch and help them tide over their problems. The population of Edfu had reached that point in their existence where they couldn't be bothered with who their nomarch was. Anyone who could put food in their bellies and clothes on their backs, and was willing to straighten out the matters would be happily anointed as their new nomarch.

But the banks were clear. The throngs that he had expected weren't there; instead, a small welcoming party comprising the high officials of the state was there to receive him. It was odd, but he played along. Politics was quite like *senet*, and in the one night that he had spent with her, he had learned that Ashayt knew all the moves.

Inside the nomarch's residence, everything appeared normal. Ankhtifi had a feeling that inside the harem, there might even be an atmosphere of celebration. If Khuy used to treat all his women the same way he treated Ashayt, it would be impossible to find anyone mourning his death.

After they crossed the work-chambers, the audience hall, and the courtyard, and reached the entrance of the harem, Ankhtifi was escorted inside by a maid, while others stayed behind.

His mouth was dry and his heart thundered under his ribs. He felt like a young boy of sixteen, nervous with anticipation. It amazed him that he didn't trip and fall as he followed the maid up the steps that led into the living quarters of the dead nomarch.

When the maid pushed the curtains aside for him to enter, he was struck with such awe that for a moment he forgot everything, including the purpose of his visit.

He had heard the stories about the wealth and riches that Khuy had amassed, but he had never imagined that Khuy's own living quarters would be richer than Pharaoh's. The walls of the chamber were adorned with expensive woolen carpets that had scenes of hunts, horses, chariots, and palaces. The carpets overlapped with one another, ensuring that not a speck of white could be seen through. Short pilasters dotted the room, each carrying bowls of fruits and decanters of wine. The low seats on both sides of the room, were gilded and gemmed, and the sled-tables had centerpieces made of ivory. Everything in the room was crafted to perfection.

"Are you going to stand there and make me wait for another seventeen years?" Ashayt implored him from the door. She stood there, dressed in white linen, with lilies in her hair. He found that oddly endearing. Lilies were for brides not for widows, so he knew that she had worn them for him.

He walked up to her and scooped her in his arms. She was surprisingly light for her age, and Ankhtifi was incredibly strong for his, so he effortlessly carried her into the bedchamber.

The bedchamber was as artfully decorated as the living chamber, and the bed was covered with sheets of silk, but now Ankhtifi couldn't be bothered with appreciating any of it. He lay her down on the bed, then reached out and tore her thin robe away, leaving her clad only in the faience pectoral and the gold waistband.

"Your absence has tortured me enough," he rasped, his voice now controlled by his burning desire to unite with her.

Ashayt flung her arms around his neck and pulled him to her, his need demanding and pulsating against her belly. She reached out for the clip that held the belt he wore and then pulled away the fabric that separated them. Their passion mounted and melted, and then finally rose to erupt inside her, again and again, with the violence of a volcano that finds release after simmering for tens of thousands of years.

In those last throes of passion, Ankhtifi heard the giggles. Spent and still buried within her, he felt his passion slipping away. He pulled himself out and turned to locate the source of those giggles.

"Again, do it again," hissed the dwarf with his mad popping eyes riveted to Ankhtifi's naked torso.

Ankhtifi looked at Ashayt who was covering herself up, unperturbed by the rude interruption.

"Why is he still here?" he demanded.

The troll replied, pointing his fat misshapen finger to his chest, "I am here, because I am the new nomarch. Lord Simonthu, ruler of the nome of Edfu and husband of…"

Before he could complete his sentence, Ankhtifi's

hands had wrapped themselves around his neck, squeezing it, making sweat break across the dwarf's forehead as he gasped for breath.

Ankhtifi's anger was rare – rarer than rain in Egypt, but the idiot had gone too far. Ankhtifi's lips were stretched so tight that Ashayt could see the impression of his teeth through them, his eyes were half-closed, and his knuckles had turned white.

"Ankhtifi, wait," she cried, but fell silent when he held out his hand.

His fingers clasped around the halfwit's throat, tightening and making him gasp for breath. Then he lifted him off the ground. Simonthu, the new nomarch of Edfu was hanging from the fist of Ankhtifi, his eyes and his tongue hanging out and his feet kicking under him.

"Let my husband down at once," Ashayt screamed, "or I will kill you!"

Her husband?

He couldn't believe he had heard right. After all these years, they had found each other, and now there was nothing that could've stopped them from marrying, and yet, she had thrown it all away.

He looked at her and then at the finger-long copper knife that she was holding to his throat.

She was serious about the troll.

He let him fall to the ground, where he lay squirming until Ashayt called her maid and had him removed.

Then they talked, and he understood.

~~~ 𓊪 𓊪 𓊪 ~~~

Ankhtifi sat on the deck of the barge with the pendant clasped in his fist. His fingers moved over the faience-studded wings of the scarab and then rolled upon the burnished carnelian sun that it held in its pincers, as he watched the buildings on the bank of Nile roll past.

The pendant was a reminder that he could love and lose, and yet win.

Edfu couldn't find a better governor than Ashayt that much was clear. She loved Edfu, and the people of Edfu respected her. With the halfwit as her husband, she could help her nome.

As the barge floated past the nomarch's residence, he heard the bell toll.

Now Edfu's complaints would be heard.

Edfu was saved.

ᴡᴡᴡ 𓈖 𓈖 𓈖 ᴡᴡᴡ

Historical Notes:

During the First Intermediate Period, when Egypt was divided into Upper Egypt (ruled from Thebes) and Lower Egypt (ruled from Henen-nesut (Herakleopolis,) Ankhtifi, the Governor of Nekhen (later called Hierakonpolis,) had aligned himself to the rulers of Lower Egypt.

Upper Egypt, at the time of Ankhtifi, was experiencing the rule of a string of weak Pharaohs, which in the course of time, would be broken by Mentuhotep the Second, who would once again unify all of Egypt.

For a short period of time, Ankhtifi did bring the nome of Edfu under his governance, but the length of time for which he controlled it, isn't clear.

Story Five

THE KEEPER OF SECRETS

~ | New Kingdom | ~

THE KEEPER OF SECRETS

Anen stopped chiseling the image of his lord and owner upon the false door of the subterranean tomb's wall, and took a long deep breath. Sculpting was hard work, but unlike painting, it produced a lot of noise, especially when the material was quartzite. The rat-a-tat of the hammer upon the head of the chisel drowned the other sounds that anyway wouldn't have reached the ground above, but he couldn't take the risk. It was time that he got out of here and left for Thebes.

He stepped back and looked at the profile of Senenmut that he had carved upon the door. The side-face of Senenmut, his lord, the Master Builder and the Chief Architect of this site, could be identified by the characteristic furrow that ran down from the sides of his nose to his chin. Despite his anguished state, Anen had done a good job of carving the face.

He backed away from the wall and sat down upon the stone stool letting the chisel and the hammer clatter to the floor. The muffled sound of her screams had now stopped completely and there was no need for him to continue hammering. The need for the camouflage had ceased to exist.

The false door was a threshold between the worlds of the living and the dead. It served as a passageway for the *ka* or spirit of the dead. Despite the grimness that enveloped his own soul today, an ironical smile crossed Anen's face. The dead was indeed on the other side, and when the *ka* of Senenmut would finally cross over, there shall be a reunion of two spirits that neither would have expected.

The moment appeared unreal to him as he sat upon the stool, clutching its edge and trying to still his shivering fingers. His eyes went back to the edge of the false door. The slab fit snug and it was impossible for a layman or even a mason to see that it had been removed and fixed again.

But Anen wanted to be sure, so he lifted one of the two oil-lamps and checked the edges of the door in its light. They looked fine, almost pristine.

He wiped his brow with the back of his hand and picked up the water-skin. The water bearer had come in an hour ago, but Anen was too nervous to have turned and looked anyone in the eye, so he had kept to his work. Thankfully, the water-skin was full. He swung it to his lips and guzzled the water down greedily. The water flooded his insides and rejuvenated him just the way the river flooded each year to rejuvenate the land of Egypt.

Inside the tomb, more than seventy cubits under the earth, it was impossible to tell the time but at least six hours must have passed since dawn. The royal procession would have already left. He should have been there with all other artists, sculptors, masons, and workers, biding their Pharaoh farewell. He hoped and prayed that his absence wasn't noticed.

Djeser Djeseru, sublime of the sublimes, the under-construction mortuary temple of Pharaoh would be deserted right now. The white light of the afternoon sun would make the temple complex look divine and bright. It was the beginning of *Peret*, the season of planting, and the winter was just about to set in.

The thought filled Anen with a strange longing. The temple compound had been his home for more than a decade, and now, he will have to leave it, forever.

Anen emptied the whole skin, gulping down its contents greedily – not just to quench his thirst, but also to cleanse his soul. *If only he could undo what he had done.* Inside the tomb the air was heavy with the smell of damp earth, sweat, and death.

He was hit by a sudden wave of claustrophobia adumbrated by guilt, and all he wanted to do was get out. A lot of things needed to be done. He had to get to Thebes as soon as he could, and then hope that he would be able to meet Pharaoh's eunuch.

Just three days ago, everything was different. Three days ago, Anen's biggest worry was whether his work would please Pharaoh.

~~~ 𓈖 𓈖 𓈖 ~~~

Pharaoh was arriving the next morning and Anen was still unsure if the relief in the south colonnade of the middle court would meet Pharaoh's approval.

The royal entourage would first visit the temple of Amun on the east bank. Pharaoh went there every year after the planting and made offerings to the god so that Egypt may be blessed with a plentiful harvest. Then she would visit the site of her mortuary temple, *Djeser Djeseru.*

Djeser Djeseru was ensconced in the lap of the new necropolis. The old one with the pyramids was at Sakara. This was the place that Akhenaten the heretic king had chosen to be his portal into afterlife. While the pharaohs who followed Akhenaten did their best to obliterate all traces of his mono- theistic religion and revert to the old ways and to the cult of Amun, they followed the road that Akhenaten had taken to the afterlife. Since his time, the tombs of the pharaohs were dug in these great mountains that towered over the west bank of the Nile. The limestone cliffs were the perfect hideout for the dead royalty – They kept the tombs hidden from the public eye, the mummies of the pharaohs safe from desecration, and their treasures secure from the tomb-robbers. The mortuary temples of the pharaohs, however, were places where their family members and subjects could pray for their souls, and so they were grand, accessible places, each with its own priests who maintained the temple and managed its affairs.

Among the mortuary temples that stood on the west bank, *Djeser Dejseru* was the grandest. While it was built upon an unfinished temple of Akhenaten, little remained of that earlier monstrosity with those elongated alien figures. The temple now looked different from anything that Egyptians had laid their eyes upon ever before. The beauty and precision of its colonnaded structure could only be compared to that of the pyramids – nothing else could even come close.

Pharaoh Hatshepsut's mortuary temple was made of three courts and two colonnades and it faced the temple of Pharaoh's patron god Amun Ra, which was situated across the Nile, upon its east bank. The entrance was through a ramp that cut right through the middle of the Punt garden and ascended to the first colonnade, which leveled with the second court. Another ramp began in the second court and rose to the level of the second colonnade, where turning left would present one with scenes from the expedition to Punt – these scenes were painted by Anen and other artists; and on the right was the birthing colonnade, which established that Pharaoh was indeed the daughter of Amun and was helped into this world by different gods and goddesses. The third and the upper court would later have the temples of Pharaoh's cult and of Amun Ra, but so far the plan was only on papyri and all that was there now was Anen's tent, perched upon a flat horizontal clearing on the limestone cliff behind.

The day before Pharaoh's visit, Anen was working in the Punt colonnade. The whole place was laid with papyrus mats and the air was heavy with the smell of paints mingling with the smell of sweat that sparkled upon the brows and shoulders of the artists. But there was more in the air than just these smells; there were rumors and speculations too. Everyone was talking about Pharaoh's impending visit. It was her third visit in the last ten years, and from the last visit, only a few artists were still working here.

"Wait till tomorrow and you'll see for yourself. Our Pharaoh is a man." He heard a new apprentice quip. The new apprentices were taught to draw a different, more masculine visage of Pharaoh, and most of them had not seen Pharaoh in person, so Anen wasn't surprised. He too had never seen her up close, but Senenmut's descriptions of Pharaoh were lucid enough to tell him that their Pharaoh was indeed a woman.

After the fourth hour in the afternoon, the conversations and jokes usually began to turn ribald. Most of the workers would leave the site and head toward the caves that riddled the limestone cliffs behind. The site workers used these caves for rest and recreation.

While they slept out in the open, or in tents pitched near the site, inside these caves the artists, sculptors, stonecutters, masons, even the occasional travelers, sought and found pleasures of the body, both real and vicarious. They brought with them, flasks of *heqt* that they shared, along with stories, real and imaginary.

Some sat there and talked about the lives they had left behind, but most would tell stories of violence and lust, spiced up to titillate the listeners. Every ten days, the workers got a day off from work, and while most preferred to stay back and rest, the adventurous ones would leave and return to recount their experiences in the pleasure-houses of Thebes. Those who never left the site came to the caves in search of such psychological aphrodisiacs that would help them release the tensions pent up in their bodies, for there were hardly any women on the site.

The most popular of these caves and the one nearest to *Djeser Djeseru* was the Cave of Atem.

Anen hadn't visited the cave for a whole year, because he hadn't felt the need. He would not have gone there last week too, had his co-worker, Ipy the sculptor, not pulled him along.

"You know Menhru?" he had asked Anen, drawing him to a corner.

Anen had a faint recollection of the man Ipy was talking about. He remembered an adventurous young artist, who found it difficult to stick to the traditional rendering of the human body.

"The artist who asked Senenmut why we must draw a boy as a grown man, only smaller in size?" he offered.

"Yes, the same," Ipy had nodded vigorously. "Menhru has been working on a set of twelve pictures, and on papyrus too. His drawings show more than you can ever imagine. You must see them or your life will be drier than the western desert," he told him.

There is nothing that I can't imagine or that I haven't experienced, he had thought then. He must have blushed having remembered some of it, because Ipy had noticed it. He and Ipy were friends too, and though Anen had never shared his innermost thoughts with him, Ipy could often read his face.

"You aren't sipping out of the Master Builder's cup, are you?" he had enquired, lifting one of his brows to throw him a hint about Meryekre.

Anen had shoved him away, feigning amusement, but to set Ipy's doubts to rest, he had gone along. Since then, a million times he had wished that he hadn't. *But if I hadn't, I would have never known,* thought Anen.

His anxiety suddenly shot up. It was time for him to go because between tonight and tomorrow morning, he would learn the truth.

Anen carefully placed his palette down upon the makeshift pilaster that he had built by placing one block of stone over the other, and walked out to the middle-court to check the sundial. The fourth hour of the afternoon had already passed, which meant that in about an hour it would be dark. The air outside was already beginning to cool down. The tall cliffs that loomed behind the temple in the west had hidden the setting sun and enveloped the whole compound in their cool shadow.

Inside the colonnade, artists were applying the last coat of paint to the series of reliefs that told the story of the Punt expedition. The expedition was one of the important highlights of Pharaoh's rule, and it was important that every little detail was brought out with dazzling clarity. Twenty artists, both relief sculptors and painters, were busy with their chisels and paintbrushes. Soon they would put it all away and go back to their dreams and nightmares, though none shall be as vivid or heartbreaking as his.

After everyone left, an odd silence would descend upon the site – a silence broken only by the heavy footfall of the six guards that secured the site as Senenmut's personal domain. The guards would pace up and down outside the Punt garden in the lower court.

Anen was the only one who slept on the site. His small tent set at the mouth of a shallow cave held his few possessions, which he knew were worth nothing if he ever needed to sell them, but then he was Senenmut's slave and his responsibility. He had come here, a boy of twelve, wearing a rag that barely covered his nakedness. Scared and lost, he had attached himself to a caravan of unemployed men and women who had traveled from the Delta in hope of finding work.

It was now the seventeenth year of Pharaoh Hatshepsut's rule, and the construction of *Djeser Djeseru* had begun ten years ago. Since then, Anen had risen from being a stone chipper to a draftsman who assisted Senenmut, the Master Builder, by drawing and painting his ideas on stone-plates and later on papyri.

Anen would never have become a senior draftsman had Senenmut not caught him drawing upon the very stones he was supposed to be chipping. Since then, he had been under Senenmut's tutelage, learning from him skills that were denied to a slave. He had not only learned to write but to measure and to calculate, yet his most important strength still lay in drawing what Senenmut wanted him to draw. Quite the raconteur, Senenmut would describe every little detail with such vividness that Anen was driven to draw it all then and there, bringing alive Senenmut's imagination and expressing it upon either stone or papyri for all to see.

Anen looked at the sundial and decided that he didn't want to return to work that evening. Instead he ran up the steps to the upper court, his *shenti* flapping against his thighs and the soft evening breeze pushing through his locks, caressing his scalp like his mother who was now but an unreal wisp of memory.

He climbed the steps that he had himself cut out in the rock, and flicked open the flap to his own miserable hovel of a tent. His dwelling was a curious place – a tent in the front but a shallow cave at the back. A rolled up papyrus mattress and a few drawings were stacked against the limestone wall. A small wooden box sat on the floor, upon which lay a polished copper plate - a trinket he had found half buried in the sand, a piece of treasure that a tomb-raider or a rich person had lost. He had shown it to Senenmut who had allowed him to keep it. The plate, he had realized as he grew up, solved another purpose.

When polished, it showed him his reflection. So he had taken to burnishing it daily. He hadn't been this vain before, not until she had told him that he was beautiful.

Anen picked up the plate and peered at his reflection. For the last whole year, it had been beaming back at him - his eyes sparkling, his cheekbones strong above the dimples that his smile cast upon both his cheeks, and his hair dark and oiled. He stood the mirror upon the box, and walked back, trying to get as much of himself into the mirror as he could. He couldn't see his face now, but his broad shoulders, his muscled chest, and his tight stomach now filled the plate's expanse.

For the last whole year, he had been meeting her once every moon, and before he went to meet her, he always looked at himself in the mirror, but today it was different. Today, his reflection scowled at him, his straight nose had flared nostrils and his full lips were pursed. It was the reflection of an unhappy man.

Anen slipped down to the ground and sat with his back against the wall and his feet spread out in front of him. Everything that Anen possessed was given to him by Senenmut - the rings that he kept in the leather pouch under his clothes, the papyrus rolls, the brushes, the amulets, even that little alabaster container. Unlike the days of the pyramids, about half the workers in Egypt now were slaves, and yet, Senenmut had treated him more like a ward than a slave.

Everything I have is Senenmut's…
He shook his head.
My love is mine – I didn't take it from anyone.

〜〜 𓏤 𓏤 𓏤 〜〜

It was dusk when he entered the Master Builder's tent, which was set to the east of the middle courtyard, right next to the birthing colonnade.

Unlike Anen's own miserable hovel, Senenmut's tent was a grand affair. It had an antechamber complete with a big table in the center, around which were cushioned stools. Here, often in the evenings, Senenmut met with the senior artists and sculptors to discuss the administrative issues.

The antechamber was separated from the bedchamber by heavy curtains imported from the north. Nobody had seen Senenmut's bedchamber – except Anen, and he too hadn't seen it until about a year ago.

Oil lamps that burned steadily with their flames enclosed inside glass bowls were placed upon pilasters around the antechamber, and candles burned in the candelabra that stood in the center of the big table. The copper candelabra were shaped in the form of a woman carrying a bowl of fragrant water upon her head. As the candles around the woman burned, it warmed the water in the bowl, exuding a soft, bewitching fragrance that weakened the smell the oil and tallow, and filled the chamber with an air of expectancy.

Tonight, Senenmut's antechamber wasn't prepared to receive his team. Instead it was prepared to receive *a lover*.

Anen crossed the length of the antechamber and reached the entrance of the bedchamber. Since the summer of the sixteenth year of Pharaoh Hatshepsut's rule, they had availed of every opportunity that Senenmut's absence provided, and yet he hadn't developed the temerity to enter Senenmut's bedchamber on his own. He stood there, waiting for the curtains to part and for her to invite him in.

Standing there, Anen always felt like what he was - a

slave waiting for the summons from his master – in this case, from his mistress, Meryekre.

As he waited, his thoughts took him back to the time when it had all begun.

That evening too, he had arrived in the tent of Senenmut when dusk was about to fall. He had raised the papyrus mat that covered the main entrance and entered the tent when the air outside had cooled down and the lamps had been just lighted, coloring the mood of the hour in the hues of mauve romance.

The workers had already left and the servants were busy in the kitchens outside the temple grounds. The only people who usually remained on the site in evenings were the engineers and the artists who wanted to discuss their plans and drawings with Senenmut.

In his excitement of having visualized a very complex scene that displayed the Egyptian ship being loaded with its exotic cargo at Punt, Anen had forgotten that Senenmut had left the site in the afternoon and gone to Thebes where he would meet Pharaoh and settle the affairs of worker-payments with the treasurer. Whenever Senenmut went to Thebes he stayed the night there. Among the workers, rumors abounded that Senenmut had a somewhat risqué reason to spend his nights there, but none of these rumors ever reached Senenmut. Regardless of their position on the site, everyone knew how great a penalty such rumormongering could evoke.

That evening, when he had entered Senenmut's tent, hoping to consult with his mentor, the empty antechamber had immediately reminded him of his error. He had turned to leave, when he heard the soft sound of a woman crying. It came from the living quarters. The sound made him curious so emboldened by the Master Builder's absence, Anen had tiptoed to the curtains of the bed-chamber and parted them a little to peep inside. He was taken aback when Meryekre smiled at him from across the room.

She looked right into his eyes. Her makeup looked perfect, untouched by the tears that he had imagined. Wearing a thin sheath of white linen she was lying on the low red couch that stood against the foot of the bed. Her linen sheath had a golden border, which sparkled under her soft garnet tipped breasts. A thin chain of gold glimmered around her neck. Her complexion, a beautiful light brown, had the warmth of Egypt and the calm of the north; her face glowing golden with a coppery sheen looked ethereal, her eyelids painted with green malachite and lined with black galena held the key to the mysteries that until then were a forbidden dream for young Anen. Her red lips were curved in an inviting smile. Lying there, she looked like a goddess.

Anen's eyes slid from her face to her full breasts then moved along the line of her slim waist, and ran across her flaring hips and sculpted thighs – the pylons guarding the entrance to paradise.

He had stood there behind the curtains, the way he was standing now, mesmerized, until she had risen from the couch and walked toward him, her hips undulating, her breasts shaking ever so slightly but enough to make him want to touch them and feel their softness.

As he watched her, he felt himself rise and swell, quite like the Nile before the inundation. Somewhere, in the mists of his thoughts, he heard a warning that the woman was probably Senenmut's half-sister. While pharaohs were gods and they could wed their own siblings, the common man followed a different set of traditions. Senenmut, of course, wasn't a traditional man, and yet it was impossible to say what relationship he had with her. He had heard the rumors – but rumors weren't always true.

It didn't matter. Whether he slept with Senenmut's mistress or deflowered his master's sister – in both cases, he would be treading dangerous grounds. That Senenmut would pardon such a crime, even if the perpetrator were his favorite artist, was impossible to imagine. Every single fiber in his body understood how big a risk it would be and yet demanded that he ignored it.

Meryekre was half of Senenmut's age – young, about nineteen. Swaying her body like a snake dancing to the tunes of a snake charmer, she reached him and yanked the curtain aside. Anen remembered that without the curtain covering his body, he had suddenly felt naked, for his stele had pushed so hard against his shenti that the linen had tightened to reveal his excitement to her. She continued to come closer, until her breasts were pressed against his chest and her belly against his excited and aroused member.

They hadn't spoken at all. There had been no introduction, no conversation. She took his hand and led him to the bed. No words passed their lips. There was no other sound except their low groans of desire and erotic squishes of their perspiring bodies moving against each other, followed by their cries of ecstasy when he entered her. They crashed into each other again and again; breaking all barriers and helping each other experience the peak of pleasure that, until then, hadn't existed for them. The smell and sound of their need mingled with that of their excitement as they climaxed together, after which they lay panting upon Senenmut's bed.

As they lay there, side-by-side, their fingers entwined and their skins glistening from the labor of their passionate lovemaking, Meryekre turned her side to face him and propped her head on her hand.

"Anen," she murmured running a hennaed finger across his chest, "I waited for three long years."

He didn't reply. As his breathing normalized and his head cleared, he remembered his discovery.

"You are not a virgin," he asked her but repented immediately. It was not his place to ask her such a question.

Meryekre was nonplussed. Instead of feeling offended, she bent over his mouth, opened it with her tongue and kissed him deep. Then she drew away and laughed.

"Did you expect me to be a virgin? Don't you listen to the rumors? They are truer than you can imagine," she said and then enquired light-heartedly. "Do virgins invite strange men into their beds?"

He saw her smile vanish giving way to a glimpse of pain on her face.

For a moment, Anen felt a rush of jealous rage shoot up through his gut and trickle into his heart. The jealousy was irrational. She wasn't his to keep – she belonged in the household of his master. He had no right to ask the question, but it just popped out.

"Who was he?"

She raised herself up and pulled the linen on the bed to cover her naked body. Then she turned to him and said slowly, in a calm but resigned tone.

"He still is and will always be. Anen, please don't speak about it to anyone," she had pleaded.

"About us?"

She had given him a long desperate look – the look of a jailed bird, of a gazelle caught in a hunter's net - and then whispered.

"About us, and about him and me."

He had spent that night in her bed. Learning from her the methods of seeking and providing pleasure. He hadn't slept a wink that night, and yet when the day dawned, he had found himself brimming with energy. The golden rays of the rising sun filled him with hope, and the twittering of the birds from the Garden of Punt in the lower court of the temple complex, made his heart soar. Everything had come alive around him. He felt it all with more passion - the texture of the stone beneath his fingers, the smell of the colors he ground, the warmth of the breeze, the taste of the food he ate – he felt it all, and in doing so, he felt more alive than ever.

The next morning when he had returned to work, his life was no longer mundane. His step was lighter, his heart was aflutter, and he couldn't stop himself from looking at Senen-mut's tent whenever he could. Even looking at Senenmut's tent from afar would make him stiffen below the belly and under his *shenti*, for the night would replay in his mind again and again, making his memories of it more vivid and crisp, the way a painting would become richer and crisper with each new layer of color.

His face would abruptly break into a smile when his hands were busy painting because his mind wandered away, carrying him outside the colonnade, across the middle court, into Senenmut's bedchamber, lying next to her, their skins touching, then burning from the touch.

He remembered how Ipy had seen him blush and smile when he was painting the obese wife of the Punt chief, and cracked a crass joke about how even that ugly hag would pound him to pulp if he tried his luck with her.

Today, it all felt like another lifetime to him. He was here, in Senenmut's tent once again, and his heart should have been racing in happy anticipation, but it wasn't.

Anen stood there rooted to his place behind the curtain, remembering the days gone by. Over the course of the year, it had become a game between them. They were still waiting for the time when Anen would walk into the bedchamber without being asked in, but he couldn't. He was a slave and would remain one until he could buy his freedom. It was odd that in the last whole year, he hadn't once thought about freedom... *until now.*

His reverie was broken when she pulled the curtains open to admit him in. Today she wore a pleated skirt made of the thinnest linen dyed the color of wine. It fell from her shoulders and cascaded down her breasts and belly to cover her thighs, faintly outlining the triangle between them.

"Why do you always stop outside? It has been a whole year now and you still wait for me to come and bring you inside, why Anen?"

He had no answer to her question. She couldn't understand how being a slave could bind a man in invisible chains.

"Because I can't," he replied laconically and allowed himself to be pulled across the bedchamber to the bed. He sat on the edge – for an odd, recently acquired reason, he didn't want to make love tonight.

"What's wrong?" she asked, pushing him down on the bed – her hands softly finding their way under his *shenti*.

He caught her hand and pushed it away. The anger in his action wasn't lost on her.

"Why?" she asked, puzzled by the violence she felt in

him.

"Who is he?" he demanded.

"You know who he is," she replied, her eyes widening. He saw fear shining through them. In the year past, they had made love and talked about love. She had told him that she didn't love that wrinkled brute but since he was a dangerous man who couldn't be denied, she had to keep up appearances. She had also told him about her past and how Senenmut had given her family a tract of prime arable land in Memphis, and pulled them out of destitution. She was honor-bound to serve him, and in that manner, she was Senemut's slave too – a slave without a scroll of ownership stamped by the authorities.

And so Anen too had learned to accept his lord as the man who he must share Meryekre with, but this was different.

Anen pushed himself up from the bed and walked across the chamber to her *ankh*-table and opened the alabaster jar that he had painted for Senenmut three years ago. Only then he hadn't known that it was meant for Meryekre.

He removed its lid, took out her galena stick and brought it back to the bed where Meryekre sat. She had regained her lost composure, but she still looked anxious. Anen sat down on the bed beside her, then took her hand and opened her fist.

"Anen, what are you doing?" she enquired, confused and anxious.

"Nothing," he replied.

She had no reason to be anxious, not if Khusebek had been lying. In the Cave of Atem, workers lied all the time. They boasted of their imaginary exploits with women of noble birth, for such stories stimulated envy, making the tellers of the stories the center of attraction.

Upon her open palm, he drew the face that he had seen in the cave. It was the face that had filled his nights with misery and his days with anger. When he had finished drawing it, he suddenly looked at Meryekre's face, giving her no opportunity to compose herself.

Before she could gather herself and put on her beautiful, ravishing smile, he saw her blanch.

"Who is this?" she asked him, turning her palm to see the face better. But he had seen her expression before she had regained control of her emotions, and he knew that the expression would now forever remain frozen in his memories.

"It was meant to be a self-portrait. But I must have drawn a terrible one, or you would have recognized it," he parried, rubbing her palm with his thumb to erase the drawing, as he mourned his lost first love and agonized upon his future as Senenmut's favorite artist.

She gave him a bewitching smile and reached up under his *shenti* once again. He felt nothing at first, but then his body began to respond and yet his heart ached from the pain caused by the sword of hatred twisting and turning inside it. He had trusted her, when she had told him that she loved him – and he had given her his life. He was willing to kill his dream of freedom and remain Senenmut's slave all his life, so that he could be close to her. But that was until he hadn't seen her recognize Khusebek in his drawing on her palm.

That night, their lovemaking was energetic and demanding, but laced with a streak of violence that had never been there before. His actions were filled not with the warm energy of love, but fueled by an anger that had welled inside his heart, which now pumped through his veins, forcing him to hurt her. He slowed down when he heard her sobs because a thin sliver of memory that reminded him of his love for her, refused to fade away, but then his imagination threw at him the images of her with Khusebek, and in the wild throes of pleasure, his anger returned, white and hot, spurting out of him and scalding her, as he kept pounding into her, working himself into a frenzy, until the clamor in his head turned into a deafening roar followed by an agonizing silence.

They collapsed upon the bed - he spent and she broken. She was still under him, her face streaked with tears. She kept sobbing with her eyes closed. A faint realization that he had caused her pain, struggled to reach his consciousness.

I should apologize, he thought, but with a shock he realized that he didn't care anymore.

~~~ 〳 〳 〳 ~~~

The morning of Pharaoh's visit was a tumult of gilded visions. The unruly crowds trying to touch Pharaoh so that some of her immortality may rub onto them, the din of drums and harps that played the marching music for Pharaoh's cavalcade, the riot of smells that emanated from bodies perfumed and unwashed alike, all worked together to transform the deserted west bank and make it buzz with activity.

Many who owned skiffs and boats had crossed the Nile to arrive at the temple, the same as the riffraff who rode the public barges and piled upon the bank half a mile away. They came for the free food that would be distributed in the evening. Even the dogs from the streets of Thebes had followed the beggars and the bums to the west bank, where they basked in the morning sun and rolled on the ground, waiting for the Feast of Pharaoh to begin.

Pharaoh Hatshepsut, wore the red and white double crown of Egypt upon her brow, and rode in a ceremonial chariot pulled by four roan horses. It had a golden sunburst upon the guard, and it displayed scenes from the hunts and the court upon its sides. The chariot, due to its ceremonial nature was about double the size of those used in military. Pharaoh sat upon a cushioned throne with Neferure, her daughter, by her side.

This was the first time that Anen had seen Pharaoh

Hatshepsut, and to him, she didn't appear to be as beautiful as she looked in the scenes he had painted or the sculptures in the workshop. She was shorter than the average Egyptian woman, but the double-crown made her look taller. A portly woman, she looked quite unlike the pictures of her that he had painted for posterity. Her face was painted white, her lips red, and her eyes were outlined in black. She wore pleated robes that covered her breasts and were held in place with a gem-studded gold pectoral. Although some of the sculptors had received new reference sketches from Thebes that showed her with a false beard and a rather masculine built, she was clearly a woman.

Anen knew that Pharaoh's visit had two purposes, the first of which was already fulfilled. She had been to the temple of Amun on the east bank, and dedicated the two obelisks – one to her father and the other to God Amun. After the ceremony there, the procession that included Pharaoh seated upon her throne in the royal chariot, other charioteers, horse-riders, infantry men, and the staff had all got on the barge, which was rowed by a hundred men and was brought to the west bank to her own mortuary temple. She was here to inspect the works.

As he stood there in the crowd of the workers, watching the procession go by, Anen prayed and hoped that Pharaoh would like his renderings of her.

He believed that Pharaoh's judgment would be influenced by her vanity, for she was after all, a woman. For an instant he felt grateful that the artists and the sculptors were required to render the royals in an idealized form, identifying them through symbols and hieroglyphs instead of their features, for he was sure that a realistic rendering of Pharaoh Hatshepsut's visage had the potential of making her terribly angry and resulting in a tragic outcome for the poor artist.

As the procession rolled forward through the exotic

Garden of Punt in the lower court and moved toward the middle-court, all the artists, including Anen, clamored to get back to their work, so that when Pharaoh arrived they were all at their workbenches tinkering away. Senenmut had instructed that they should all be present when Pharaoh arrived for she may want to speak to them.

Inside the temple complex, they waited for Pharaoh's arrival. The sculptors had spent the entire morning polishing their sculpting tools, which were now laid out upon their workbenches. The artists had cleaned their color-grinders, palettes, and brushes, and arranged everything in a vibrant display of blues, reds, greens, whites, and yellows. They stood at their spots and waited, doing nothing substantial. The sculptors were chipping away stone from the unimportant areas of the reliefs they were working on, and the artists were busy mixing colors instead of applying them. All of them were strung tight, because between the nod and shake of Pharaoh's head, lay their destiny.

After an interminable wait, Anen saw Pharaoh's throne being carried up the ramp. Among the officials that accompanied Pharaoh, was Senenmut, clad in the whitest linen, wearing around his neck the medallions with his important titles, including the most prestigious one – High Steward of the King, the one that was bestowed upon him by Pharaoh Hatshepsut. An artist had once remarked that Senenmut must have been born looking old, and so when he would actually age, nobody would know the difference. He was right. Now, in his late forties, Senenmut looked younger than his years. True, his face was deeply lined, but his eyes were sharp, his neck muscular, and he had just a hint of a double chin. Senenmut walked on the right side of Pharaoh, a step behind the Chief Vizier, his gaze piercing through the deep shadows of the colonnades, silently ordering them all to get back to work and put up a show worthy of Pharaoh.

Anen, like the others, followed Senenmut's unpro-nounced order and turned his attention to his work. When Pharaoh would enter the South colonnade of the middle court, he would start painting the baboon. He checked his palette of colors and his brushes once again.

Pharaoh's interest was mainly in the north and south colonnades of the middle court, and the reason wasn't difficult to surmise. The north colonnade told the story of Pharaoh Hatshepsut's birth and the south colonnade depicted scenes from the seven-year-long Egyptian voyage to the distant land of Punt – it was Pharaoh's pet project and the only trade voyage to be sent that far south in the recent past.

Although he was half-expecting Pharaoh to favor Punt over the saga of her own birth, when Pharaoh entered the colonnade on foot and turned left, Anen's heart skipped a beat. Here was Egypt personified – the essence of God standing upon the same stones that he walked everyday. The thrill of the moment was tremendous, and it made his heart hammer against his chest making him feel giddy. Before he could control his racing heart, he found himself staring at Pharaoh's gold filigree sandals that covered her godly but swollen feet.

Upon hearing Pharaoh's voice, his heart lurched into his throat.

"What are you painting?" she asked in her sweet and low but regal voice.

At first he felt nervous explaining his work to her, but he quickly warmed up and took her through the entire story – from the Punt huts and their dwellers, to the chief and his obese wife, to the myrrh trees, and finally to the loading of the ship.

She listened to him intently. While she listened, Anen had an opportunity to study her features. She stood about a third of a cubit shorter than him. Her face was lined with age and her skin appeared irregular under the chalky white makeup.

Her lips were painted red with ochre. Her neck was taut, perhaps the result of the exertion needed to keep the double crown in place. Her eyes, outlined in black, were her best feature for they were the eyes of an intelligent woman. When his eyes met with Pharaoh's, he felt swayed by her power and her ability to steer events in her favor. Her eyes, he noted, had a hypnotic quality that took his attention away from her bad skin and obese body.

"Anen, I would like to discuss this again sometime," she said softly, dismissing him and moving on to the next relief.

He didn't understand what she had meant, but a slave could have his head lopped off if he attempted to question Pharaoh, so he had bowed to her respectfully and then after she had moved away, he had turned to his own work.

But something troubled him - *A face in Pharaoh's procession.* Two faces never looked so alike, not to an artist. He had seen that face somewhere. It had looked different then – unkempt and shabby with a day's worth of stubble. This face was clean-shaven.

He ignored the thought and focused on painting the baboon. He had no idea that he would be thinking about that face again, very soon.

mm 𓏤 𓏤 𓏤 mm

A temporary tent for Pharaoh was raised in the northern garden of the lower-court. The palms swung high over the tents in the *Peret* breeze, which carried the aroma from the myrrh shrubs and the frankincense trees. The trees had been brought back from Punt and planted in the garden. The seven kinds of cacti on the borders separated the court and its royal guests from the undesirable masses for whom Pharaoh's visit was an opportunity for entertainment. In the southern garden, a stage was built. The workers and their supervisors had prepared a program comprising songs, dances, and a short play to amuse Pharaoh in the evening.

What does she want from a lowly artist like me?

The thought had been torturing him relentlessly for the last many hours. He had tried to supply the answers too. *Perhaps she didn't like his rendition of the Punt expedition, or she didn't like her new, more masculine idealization that they were beginning to draw and sculpt.* And yet, he couldn't fathom why she would single him out for a discussion on any of these important matters. The artists, who were more of craftsmen, merely followed orders.

Outside the entrance to Pharaoh's tent stood armed guards with gilded headdresses and iron swords with gleaming edges. The sides of the tent were made of white and blue tightly woven fabric.

Pharaoh's eunuch accompanied Anen inside where the grandiosity of Pharaoh's makeshift tent left him flabbergasted. He had heard stories about how luxuriously the royals lived, but he had never seen anything like Pharaoh's tent ever before. Until now, for him the height of luxury was the tent of Senenmut, which when compared with this tent appeared to be the shanty.

Inside, the ground was covered with carpets and rugs that had depictions of trees, birds, animals, rivers, and mountains woven into them. The curtains were made of the silk that was imported from the land beyond Sinai. Pilasters that stood in the antechamber had bowls of water, jugs of wine, and trays of fruits upon them. His eyes stopped at another curtained entrance, which looked like it led to the inner sanctum. Anen followed the eunuch in.

Inside, Pharaoh sat upon her throne. Her swollen feet were placed in a large bowl of warm fragrant water. She had removed the double crown and was instead wearing the *nemes*.

The pectoral had also been removed and replaced by a gold chain with a pendant of the goddess Hathor. Two slave girls wearing short linen skirts gathered at the waist with faience gold belts, were sitting on the floor, massaging her feet.

When Anen entered, Pharaoh made a quick flicking gesture of her wrist and everyone, except the eunuch, left. With his heart still in his mouth, Anen fell to his knees and bent his head to touch the golden strip at the base of the throne.

Pharaoh's voice, soft and melodious, but as royal and authoritative as it was in the morning, raised him to his feet.

"You are a good artist, Anen, but are you a loyal subject?"

Anen felt a cold glob of fear slip down the nape of his neck and slide over his spine. It was a question that could be answered only in one way.

"Of course, Your Highness," he replied, without raising his eyes to look into hers.

"Look up then, look at your Pharoah, the daughter of Amun."

He raised his eyes to look at her face. Since afternoon, she had removed the white paint from her face and the red ochre from her lips. Only her eyes were still painted, and the scabs on her forehead now stood out more clearly than ever. The linen robe now on her body was much thinner than the one she had worn in the morning, and it let her corpulence settle into its folds. The *nemes* too made her look shorter and squattier. And yet, her brown eyes were as captivating as ever.

"I want you to do something for me," she said, dropping her voice to a whisper.

And then she told him.

Each word that left her lips dropped into his heart like a stone and weighed him down. The chain of his thoughts that rode upon her words bound him up and squeezed him hard, violently pushing the air out of his lungs, bringing him to the verge of collapse.

Standing there in front of Pharaoh, Anen realized that he was caught in an impossible situation. A situation that could only be resolved through treason.

It would be treason against Pharaoh to refuse, and it would be treason against Senenmut to accept. Personally, it was different today than it was the last time he had met Meryekre, or following Pharaoh's order would have been treason against his own heart too. He knew that Pharaoh's order was unequivocal and a refusal could mean a quick and possibly painful departure to the afterlife.

He bowed his head and accepted the command.

A smile spread on the royal lips. As her lips parted, they let a whiff of her godly breath escape. Even in his daze, it smelled rotten, but then perhaps it was her ungodly order that had changed his perception.

While he stood there with his head bowed and considered his predicament, the eunuch brought a papyrus roll and read out its contents. A full pardon for his deed if it was ever discovered, a commendation for the service he rendered to Pharaoh, a select tract of land by the side of Nile, and freedom from slavery – was what he would get if he did what she had asked him to do.

If only, he thought, *it didn't require me to be disloyal.*

As he stood there, listening to the eunuch, he saw the slave girls return and take their places at the feet of Pharaoh.

"Don't fail me, Anen," said Pharaoh as she dismissed him.

After the eunuch had led him out, Anen returned to his little tent on the limestone cliff. There, he sat with his back against the rough wall holding his head in his hands, reflecting upon the options available to him.

He could run away into the southern mountains and

hope that he would be able to live, or perhaps escape along the coast and find his way into the land of Punt that he had been painting all these months – but his chances of getting there alive were minimal. He could speak to Senenmut but there was no reason why he would trust him, and then it would amount to disobeying Pharaoh's command. He could have made Meryekre disappear by hiding her in a limestone cave on the other side of the cliff. He would have taken his chances and escaped with her. Her disappearance would have led Pharaoh to think that the deed was done. He could have then collected his reward, and taken Meryekre away with him.

But Meryekre didn't love him. She had used him for her pleasure and now she had found another lover. Khusebek, the dark and tall Egyptian with his bulging muscles, was her new toy. He had always thought that Meryekre loved him – but nine days ago, on their day off from work, when Ipy had wheedled him into visiting the Cave of Atem, he had learned otherwise. For the whole year past, he hadn't visited that cave, and the reason was Meryekre.

The name of the cave was a pun. Mythology had it that Atem had massaged and stroked his phallus to bring forth his seed and make Shu and Tefnut. The cave was the retreat of the sex-starved but imaginative artists and scribes who brought in shards of pottery and pieces of smoothened limestone to draw their wildest fantasies and write stories that could charge up a man so that he could follow Atem's lead. The absence of women on the site often led to other kinds of gratification and the drawings helped.

The Cave of Atem was an open secret in the valley. The pile of erotic literature in the cave had become so substantial that some of the enterprising young men had taken it upon themselves to classify the drawings and writings to help the visitors.

That evening, they had stopped at the *heqt*-shop to

get their water-skins filled, and then clambered up to the cave.
His long absence had made them curious, and he couldn't hide
behind his love for art forever. It was there in the cave, while
sharing a cup of *heqt* and listening to the raunchy jokes that
the workers cracked while the artists and the scribes drew out
their fantasies, that he had suddenly caught her name. Two
men sitting a few cubits away, with their hands under their
coarse linen kilts, were listening to a third, whose name he later
discovered was Khusebek. Khusebek was recounting his night
with the unseen one, the one who had become the fountain
of youth for the Master Builder. He went on to describe how
the fire within her burns so strong that a single man couldn't
quench it alone, and how she had held his hands and had taken
him to bed where she played with him in unimaginable ways.

Sitting in his hovel, Anen recalled that night in the
Cave of Atem and his hand curled into a fist. Khusebek's
descriptions poured into his mind like a stream of hot lava that
seared his insides as he imagined the dark muscles of Khusebek and the brown soft limbs of Meryekre writhing together
upon the same bed that he had shared with her.

Anen remembered the visceral feeling of jealousy that
had coursed through him as he had listened to Khusebek's
scurrilous stories. After spending themselves, Khusebek and
his companion had lain there for a while, talking to each other,
and that was when Anen had learned his name.

Ten days had past since, and he hadn't thought of
anything else. He was plagued with visions that sent acid shoot-
ing up his gut. *The man could be lying,* he had consoled himself,
but he needed a confirmation, *from Meryekre herself.*

And so he had asked her, and when he had seen
her blanch, he knew that Khusebek's stories were true. She
was a whore who lusted for young men, a woman who had
used him to take the edge off her desires. Now, after a year,
Anen's novelty having worn off, she needed someone else, and

Khusebek was not just any other new toy, but one that was built like a god.

He clutched his head in his hands, wondering why it felt like it would explode.

If she wanted to use him, she shouldn't have told him that she loved him. He would have happily been her toy, a plaything without emotions. Then upon being cast aside, he would not have complained. But she had not. Instead, she had made him believe that she loved him. He understood the necessity of maintaining appearances. He knew and accepted that both she and he belonged to the Master Builder, and he had made peace with it all.

And yet, she had destroyed him.

Earlier, when he looked at Senenmut's tent, his heart would fill with hope, now it filled with despair.

He shook his head. Then filled with a new purpose, he strode outside. The sky had already darkened. Below, *Djeser Djeseru* looked different tonight. Dotted with lights and fires, it looked like a bride awaiting her husband on the first night of her wedding. Far into the horizon lay the river, dark and sinewy, oddly reminding him of a cobra ready to swallow the bride's happiness and plunge her world into darkness.

A bitter smile appeared upon his lips and stayed.

Now with Pharaoh's order, he was going to gut the fire that had been consuming his insides for the past ten days. Tonight, he would meet her, and he knew just where.

A few years ago Senenmut had got three chambers constructed under the ground. They were right outside the northern boundary of the temple, and the entrance to the chambers lay very close to Senenmut's own tent. Only a few artists and masons were allowed inside, and though never told explicitly, they had surmised the purpose of those chambers. They were to be Senenmut's tomb. Meryekre and Anen had spent some close moments in that tomb, hidden from the prying eyes of a curious world.

But he would wait until the program had ended and everyone had retired for the night.

ᨓ 𒀭 𒀭 𒀭 ᨓ

Pharaoh had stayed at *Djeser Djeseru* only for that one night.

After the program was over, she retired to her tent flanked by the eunuch, her women slaves, and the officials. The princess had fallen asleep and Senemut carried her to the royal tent. Someone in the crowd had commented that he looked like "a father holding his daughter," and evoked many nervous giggles. He had heard the rumors too, and he had heard of another cave similar to the Cave of Atem, where someone had drawn a picture of Senemut and Hatshepsut in the act that could've resulted in his fathering the princess. But then the picture and the rumors would be considered blasphemous if discovered, for Pharaoh was a god too. And so the rumors were hushed and the drawing was seldom spoken of.

As Anen watched Senenmut carry the princess inside, he wondered if that drawing was based on truth. Anen was a child when Pharaoh Hatshepsut's husband Tuthmosis, second of that name, was alive and the ruler of Egypt. He had died quite young, and from what he had gathered from the grapevine, he was also very weak and ill – and some crass jokes even hinted at his impotency.

Perhaps they were lovers, for what else would make Pharaoh so angry with Meryekre?

He shrugged and began walking up the ramp. Meryekre hadn't left the tent, neither to watch the play nor to pay obeisance to Pharaoh. She was trapped inside – a bird in a golden cage. Senenmut kept her hidden from the eyes of the world – she was his little sparrow. *But then how did Pharaoh come to know of her existence?*

He missed a step and cursed. He was nervous and unsure. While he understood Pharaoh's motive, or thought he did; he still wasn't sure if he had indeed stopped loving Meryekre. *What if Khusebek wasn't speaking of her? But then why had she turned so white when he had drawn his face on her palm? Did he misread her expression?* Contradictory emotions sunk their claws into his heart and pulled at it.

He had to make his mind up and quickly too.

The middle court was deserted. The half-moon had already sailed across half the sky and yet, unlike the other days, tonight a lot of tents were lighted, but not the tent of Senen- mut. His heart went out to Meryekre. Senenmut was hiding her from Hatshepsut, and so he had ordered his tent to remain dark for the night. *She needs my help,* Anen thought, and decided to speak to her about Khusebek more clearly and demand an unambiguous answer. *Those moments that I spent with you,* his heart cried, *couldn't have all been a bundle of lies.*

He looked around to check if anyone was watching. The court was dark and deserted. A cultural program with music and dance was a rare event here on the west bank, and nobody would miss it for anything. But then he heard the rustle of fabric, the sound of a kiss, followed by quick steps, and knew that he was wrong.

Anen hid himself behind a pilaster and watched. The front flap of Senenmut's tent opened slightly. Even in the dark, there was no mistaking the dark countenance and the rippling muscles of the tall man who stepped out.

In that moment, his worst fears were confirmed and his indecision vanished.

As he opened the flap of Senenmut's tent and stepped in, Anen knew exactly what he was going to do.

ᴡᴡ 𓏤 𓏤 𓏤 ᴡᴡ

The sconces on either side of the stone staircase were kept lit all through the day, and in their flickering light, he slowly climbed out of Senenmut's secret tomb.

She had cried and sworn upon the name of every god and goddess she knew. She had promised him that she had been only his in her heart, and that she never knew Khusebek, but her pleas couldn't make him forget the scene from the Cave of Atem nor the dark figure of Khusebek slinking out of the tent. He couldn't strangulate her with her wide eyes beseeching him to let her go, so he had bound her legs and arms, and gagged her, before lifting her up and putting her into the space behind the false door.

"Why did you do it?" He had asked her through his own tears, as he had pushed the door slab in its place. She had continued to struggle in the dark hole behind the slab. He knew it because he had sat there chiseling Senenmut's figure, until the sounds of her struggle had ceased.

Halfway up the staircase, he stopped. The images that swirled in his head were torturing him. He shook his head and the images shattered and disappeared. Darkness rushed to fill the vacancy in his head.

Anen took another step but stumbled as he judged the height of the step incorrectly. He caught the wall on the side of the steps by pressing his open palm against it. Standing there, listing to a side and swaying, he tried to catch his breath.

It must be the air inside the tomb. A few more steps to fresh air, he reflected, then he ploughed on.

Outside the tomb, under the brilliant gaze of *Amun Ra,* guilt washed over him.

What have I done? He thought miserably as he stumbled out, and fell on the ground. With the sun's warmth stealing its way into his body, he wondered whether he could've done something… *anything,* differently.

For over four hours, he had been inside the dark crypt and some of its darkness had spilled into his soul. Now outside, the Egyptian sun bleached his memories of the recent events and they suddenly began feeling unreal, like they belonged in a dream. He tried to loosen his muscles and let his arms fall to his sides. As the tension left his muscles, he closed his eyes and allowed himself to feel the warmth of the sun on his face and the cool soft air on his neck and shoulders.

Upon the winter breeze rode stray notes of a song sung by a worker or a peasant, somewhere in the shadows cast by the tall cliffs behind.

> *My heart chose yours and my hands found yours,*
> *We walked together, until my heart was left alone,*
> *We walked together, until my hands were empty,*
> *And I was left wondering, if your love was ever mine…*

He knew that song, but it hadn't meant anything to him before.

> *My dreams became yours and my lips found yours,*
> *We lay together, until my dreams faded away,*
> *We lay together, until my lips lost yours,*
> *And I was left wondering, if your love was ever mine…*

The warmth of the sunlight began to give way to a strange pain, a leaden feeling in his limbs. His lips felt dry like the sand upon which he stood swaying.

Anen felt the ground under him lurch and the world around him spin. It went around him faster and faster, until he lost his balance and fell.

A figure materialized in the bright haze. A tall man, dark-skinned, his muscles reflecting the light of the sun and blinding him, strode toward him.

Anen squinted up to see his face, which shimmered and wavered like it was behind a screen of smoke. For a moment his vision cleared and he saw the face. It was the same face that he had seen in Pharaoh's procession and which he thought he had seen before.

"Khusebek?" he gurgled.

Anen tried to raise himself from the ground. He used his elbows to push himself up, but the exertion knocked the air out of his lungs. He crumpled and fell forward.

As his face hit the warm top layer of the white Egyptian sand, his eyes fluttered open.

It wasn't bright anymore.

It was dark - darker than the moonless night - even darker than the road into afterlife. He couldn't see anything. He tried to move his hands, his fingers, but he couldn't.

Why?

And then it dawned upon him.

He had been poisoned.

But how?

His parched throat wasn't letting him think. All he could think of was water and he had left his water-skin behind in the tomb.

The water-skin…the water was poisoned.

He could only hear the sound of the wind, the distant cry of an eagle, the last notes of the song, and the muffled sound of leather soles slapping the sand.

Then he heard him.

"Yes, I am Khusebek. Pharaoh's Keeper of Secrets."

᭿᭿ 𓏤 𓏤 𓏤 ᭿᭿

Historical Notes:

Senenmut is credited with building the *Djeser Djeseru*,

the mortuary temple of Queen Hatshepsut of 18th dynasty, or the Deir-el-Bahri as it is known now.

He held the titles of "Steward of the God's Wife" and "Steward of the King's Daughter".

It has been widely speculated that Senenmut and Hatshepsut were lovers, and that Hatshepsut's daughter Neferure was indeed sired by Senenmut.

An underground tomb comprising three rooms is situated quite near to the right wall of *Djeser Djeseru*, and the drawings upon the walls of this tomb have made historians conclude that the tomb was made for Senenmut, though he might have never been buried in it.

It is also speculated that Senenmut never married.

A particular painting done on the walls of a cave that the workers rested in, during the construction of *Djeser Djeseru*, shows Senenmut in congress with a woman wearing a *nemes* (assumed to be Pharaoh Hatshepsut,) is believed to be the result of rumors rife among the workers at the time.

Also by S.R. Anand

MYSTERIOUS KEMET - Book II
SEDUCTION AND CONSPIRACY
IN ANCIENT EGYPT

Now available on Amazon
https://www.amazon.com/dp/B06XRBVCYW

In this Collection, read...

I

THE RIVER BRIDE
~ | PRE-DYNASTIC PERIOD | ~

In pre-dynastic Egypt, the androgynous river god Hapi awaits his bride. As the greed of one woman collides with the desire of another, a young man tries to save the girl he loves from a lottery that has all odds stacked against her. In the tumult that ensues, a middle-aged priestess, who is caught in the conspiracy unawares, must either overcome her revulsion for a dwarf's overtures or face certain death.

II

THE NECROPHILE'S RING
~ | NEW KINGDOM | ~

The city of Thinis is undivided in its opinion. The necrophile must burn for his depravity. As the accused waits for his sentence to be carried out, three women – a love-priestess, a troubled wife, and the young daughter of an embalmer, struggle to discover the truth and find a proof that could save an innocent life.

III

THE SPINNER OF DREAMS

~ | New Kingdom – Amarna Period | ~

As Pharaoh Ay lies dying, his son Nakhtmin, the crown prince of Egypt, must either accept the crown and rule Egypt, or change Egypt's destiny by exacting an unexpected revenge from his ambitious, brilliant, but homophobic father who killed not only Nakhtmin's lover, but also his love for life.

IV

THE BREWERESS OF OMBO

~ | Ptolemaic Egypt | ~

Caught in a complex web of Roman politics, royal fratricide, and two fruitless incestuous marriages, Cleopatra must use her charisma and ingenuity to find a way to follow her secret dream, but despite all her efforts, she should pay for it with a crown and the life of a loved one.

V

THE BLUE LILY

~ | OLD KINGDOM – FIRST DYNASTY | ~

Like the other chosen ones, Mentu is destined to follow his King into the afterlife. Following the death of the King, he must place his trust in Khuit, his concubine of ten years who was once a wharf-wench. For both Mentu and Khuit, it is their only chance at life, but what is life for one, is death for the other, unless fate intervenes.

∿ 𓏏 𓏏 𓏏 ∿

MYSTERIOUS KEMET - Book II
SEDUCTION AND CONSPIRACY
IN ANCIENT EGYPT

Now available on Amazon
https://www.amazon.com/dp/B06XRBVCYW

TOGGLED

TOGGLED is a dark psychological thriller, which explores the deepest recesses of the schizophrenic mind, as it takes you from a modern day suburban neighborhood into the streets of Ancient Egypt, and then brings you back to a grim and dangerous place where death is real, but murder isn't.

Toggled...is the mind of Brice Ward.

TOGGLED on Amazon
https://www.amazon.com/dp/B06XW9KMKK

A NOTE OF THANKS

Dear Reader,

I'd like to thank you for reading "Mysterious Kemet - Book I." If you enjoyed reading it, please review it on Amazon. I shall be thankful for your kind gesture.

I've tried my best to ensure that this book doesn't contain those pesky typographical errors, yet perfection has never been my forte, so if you chance upon any, please let me know, and I'll try to correct it as soon as I can.

I would love to hear from you at SRAnand.Author@ gmail.com.

Thanks once again.

ABOUT THE AUTHOR

S.R. Anand is a storyteller who writes historical fiction, fantasy, and science fiction. When she is home, she can be found in her room, scribbling, typing, and guzzling tea; smiling at her invisible characters and driving her family mad.

When she isn't writing, she daydreams and finds herself transported to alternate worlds – historical, fantastical, or dystopian. She cannot usually stop herself from reading stories in the events happening around her and telling them, but whenever she can pull the brakes, she draws, paints, and teaches.

Her Facebook page is *facebook.com/SRAnandAuthor* and her Twitter handle is *@SRAnandAuthor*.

Printed in Great Britain
by Amazon